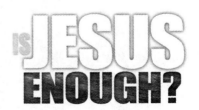

IS JESUS ENOUGH?

DAN JACKSON

IS JESUS ENOUGH?

LIVING IN THE LIGHT OF HIS LOVE

Pacific Press®
Publishing Association

Nampa, Idaho | Oshawa, Ontario, Canada
www.pacificpress.com

Cover design by Gerald Lee Monks
Cover design resources from iStockphoto.com and Dreamstime.com
Inside design by Kristin Hansen-Mellish

The author assumes full responsibility for the accuracy of all facts and
quotations as cited in this book.

Unless otherwise noted, Scripture quotations are from the HOLY BIBLE,
NEW INTERNATIONAL VERSION®, NIV® copyright © 1973, 1978, 1984,
2011 by Biblica, Inc.® Used by permission. All rights reserved worldwide.
Scriptures quoted from NKJV are from The New King James Version,
copyright © 1979, 1980, 1982, Thomas Nelson, Inc., Publishers.
Scriptures quoted from KJV are from the King James Version of the Bible.

You can obtain additional copies of this book by calling toll-free
1-800-765-6955 or by visiting http://www.adventistbookcenter.com.

Library of Congress Cataloging-in-Publication Data:

Jackson, Dan.
 Is Jesus enough? : living in the light of his love / Dan Jackson.
    pages cm
 ISBN 13: 978-0-8163-3790-3
 ISBN 10: 0-8163-3790-X
 1. Jesus Christ—Person and offices. 2. Seventh-day Adventists—
Doctrines. I. Title.
 BT203.J33 2013
 232'.8—dc23

                                    2013022734

13 14 15 16 17 • 5 4 3 2 1

Dedication

I dedicate this book to Donna,
who not only brought me to Jesus,
but who has also demonstrated through her life
that Jesus is indeed enough.

Contents

PART ONE

THE QUESTION OF SUFFICIENCY

f I have the picture right, the question of sufficiency will become more and more significant as
the time of Jesus' return draws near. The challenges
we face often bring this whole idea of sufficiency into the
center of our experience. Many of us have been trained to
think on our own, to rely on ourselves, and to have some
self-confidence. But often, when difficulties and challenges
confront us, all of this training vanishes and takes with it all
our resolve. So the question of sufficiency becomes exceedingly relevant.

As the apostle Paul contemplated the role of those who
follow Jesus in His grand, eternal procession, he asked the
question, "Who is equal to such a task?" (2 Corinthians 2:16).
There are many answers to this question. However, Paul himself, under the inspiration of the Holy Spirit, answers his own
question with great clarity: "The Son is the image of the invisible God, the firstborn over all creation. For in him all
things were created: things in heaven and on earth, visible and
invisible, whether thrones or powers or rulers or authorities;
all things have been created through him and for him. He

is before all things, and in him all things hold together. And
he is the head of the body, the church; he is the beginning
and the firstborn from among the dead, so that in everything he might have the supremacy. For God was pleased to
have all his fullness dwell in him, and through him to reconcile to himself all things, whether things on earth or things
in heaven, by making peace through his blood, shed on the
cross" (Colossians 1:15–20; see also John 3:31–36; Hebrews
1:1–3).

There is only one answer to Paul's question, and the name
of that answer is *Jesus*! He is the "All-Sufficient" One—the
One of whom Paul says, "My God will meet all your needs according to the riches of his glory in Christ Jesus" (Philippians
4:19). And in one of the most precious passages found in the
Bible, Paul asks another question and then answers it: "If God
is for us, who can be against us? He who did not spare his own
Son, but gave him up for us all—how will he not also, along
with him [that is, with Jesus] graciously give us all things?"
(Romans 8:31, 32).

Dear reader, as you journey through the pages of this
little book, I will be praying that you will discover that Jesus
can meet you right where you are today and take care of
your pressing needs. "Christ walks in the midst of the golden
candlesticks. . . . He is represented as walking, which signified
untiring wakefulness, unremitting vigilance. He observes
whether the light of any of his sentinels is burning dim or
going out. If the candlesticks were left to mere human care,
the flickering flame would languish and die. But he is the
true watchman in the Lord's house, the true warden of the

temple courts. His continued watchcare and sustaining grace are the source of life and light."[1]

Endnote

1.   Ellen G. White, *The Home Missionary*, November 1, 1893.

Chapter 1

How Much Is Enough?

Many years ago, my best friend, Lee, and I rode a Greyhound bus across two Canadian provinces in order to experience the Pacific National Exhibition in Vancouver, British Columbia. We had no particular agenda in mind; we just thought that going there was a good idea. Lee had enough money for bus fare for both of us, but little more than that, and no hotel reservations. We hadn't planned things very well at all.

Like intrepid adventurers, we set out for the exhibition early one morning, believing that a friend of ours was almost certainly working there and that he would invite us to his home for a few days. Our ambitious thoughts didn't take into account the fact that he had a mother who most likely would want to have some say regarding the invitation we assumed he would extend to us.

We spent our first night in Vancouver sleeping in newspaper bins behind the Greyhound bus terminal. However, much to our delight, the invitation did come, and we spent the next couple of nights experiencing the graciousness and generosity of those people and the comfort of their home.

On our first morning there, we were treated to a wonderful breakfast of pancakes and eggs, hot cereal, and juice. Nothing could have been better than that! Then, as we approached the end of the meal, the hostess asked, "Have you boys had enough? Would you like more?"

One would have to know a little bit of the life story of my friend Lee in order to understand what happened next. Lee had left his home while still in his teens and had found work in the oil fields of northern Alberta. He often spent his paychecks at the local bar, and frequently wound up making do for food. At times he would get so hungry that he would go into a restaurant, ask for a cup of hot water, and then pour ketchup into the cup and drink his version of tomato soup.

In other words, in those days, Lee had a healthy appetite. He was also modest, so the experience of having a full belly and being asked if he wanted more was somewhat perplexing for him. He answered with all the dignity that a seventeen-year-old could muster, "No, thank you, I have had sufficient." It was a proper retort, but unusual because of its formality, so all the young people at the table burst into laughter, and ever after "I have had sufficient" was our way of poking at one another when we thought something was being overstated.

When have you "had sufficient"? What is it that satisfies you?

Mark Zuckerberg, the cofounder and CEO of Facebook, had amassed twenty-seven billion dollars by his twenty-seventh birthday. That's a huge amount of money. Is it enough for him? Is twenty-seven billion dollars sufficient?

The question of sufficiency raises a wide variety of answers because the answers depend in part on where you live and what you're doing when the question is asked. The starving and impoverished in our world and those living in the ghettos of our cities have very different answers to these questions than do the people who live in suburban North America. And the answers are changing even within these smaller groups.

There is, however, one aspect of life in which the question of sufficiency—of what is enough—is universal. In the matter of salvation, all men and women walk on level ground. Do we humans have sufficient spiritual depth and character to deserve God's favor? Just how much is enough? And if we don't have enough, how can we get what we lack?

For me, the question then becomes, Is Jesus enough? Are His life, death, and resurrection sufficient to bring me into harmony and eternal friendship with God? Is Jesus' work of mediation for me today sufficient to enable me to face my challenges today—right now?

God Himself answers this question through the words of the apostle Paul. "He [Jesus] is able to save completely those who come to God through him, because he always lives to intercede for them" (Hebrews 7:25). In Paul's second letter to the Corinthians, he reminds us of the all-sufficiency of God's plan by reflecting to us the words of assurance that God Himself spoke to him: " 'My grace is sufficient for you, for my power is made perfect in weakness' " (2 Corinthians 12:9). In the rest of this verse, Paul tells us his response to God's assurance of His sufficiency: "Therefore I will boast all the more gladly about my weaknesses, so that Christ's power may rest on me."

There is a wonderful comment on this in an article that Ellen White wrote that was published in the May 6, 1902, issue of the *Review and Herald:* "When the attention is fastened on the cross of Christ, the whole being is ennobled. The knowledge of the Saviour's love subdues the soul, and lifts the mind above the things of time and sense. Let us learn to estimate all temporal things in the light that shines from the cross. Let us strive to fathom the depths of humiliation to which our Saviour descended in order to make man the possessor of eternal riches. As we study the plan of redemption, the heart will feel the throb of the Saviour's love, and will be ravished by the charms of his character."

The following chapters attempt to reveal the fact that Jesus is sufficient—sufficient not only to take us to heaven at the end of this world, but also to help us today. As we see Him every day, we discover that He is "a friend who sticks closer than a brother" (Proverbs 18:24).

Questions for Reflection and Discussion

1.   What's your favorite food? How much of it does it take to make you feel you've had "sufficient"? How do you know when you've had "sufficient"?

2.   What has Jesus supplied for our salvation? Is what He has supplied all that's necessary for our salvation, or must we provide something too? If so, what would that be?

3.   Ellen White wrote that when our attention is fastened on the cross of Christ, our whole being is ennobled. Why does focusing on the cross ennoble us? Earning our living and caring for the people important to us demands much of our time and energy. How then can we maintain the focus Ellen White called for?

Chapter 2

Roots: Jesus at Work

was born in Edmonton, Alberta, Canada. My father was a business agent for the Bakers and Confectioners Union. He was a self-made man: he completed only five years of formal education and then entered the workforce in order to help support his family. Through the years, he had gradually worked his way to the top position in the union.

My father was a fighter, a brawler, and a man who drank in excess. To his credit, he was also a man who didn't turn away from those who had needs. I saw him help the helpless, and on one occasion I saw him save a man's life. Unfortunately, for much of the time I spent at home, he was an alcoholic—and he was a mean drunk.

My mother had started training to become a nurse, but her dreams of a career in that profession ended tragically when she took a bad fall. Several years after her accident, my father charmed his way into her life, and she married him.

Mom was a wonderful, warm, accepting, and loving influence in the home. She was the glue that kept the family together, and along with my two sisters, Nan and Mary, I loved being around her.

Mom was a Seventh-day Adventist, but in the early stages of her marriage, she placed higher priority on my dad than on God and His church. The time came, however, when she decided that she must give God the highest priority. Her level of commitment to God and the church increased gradually at first and then exponentially. She became an avid student of the Bible, the writings of Ellen White, and Seventh-day Adventist literature. She read everything she could get her hands on written by Morris Venden and Clifford Goldstein. She kept reading, studying, and praying as long as she was able.

She was a true follower of Jesus, and she cherished the thought of His return. As a matter of fact, only a few days before she died, she voiced a question that she had asked hundreds of times before: "Has anyone seen that 'little black cloud about the size of a man's hand' in the sky?" I know that one day she'll be called from her grave and have the fabulous delight of seeing that little black cloud.

Mom's decision to make God first in her life had serious consequences within our home though. Because she attended Sabbath worship services, prayer meetings, and camp meetings faithfully and refused to compromise her faith, her commitment to God and the church became offensive to my father. As a result, Mom endured harassment and sometimes open persecution from my father.

One Friday evening, my father came home drunk and ugly. When he saw Mom reading her Bible, he became angry and began to slap her around. Eventually, he became tired and went to sleep. When he did, Mom called us children together and we fled—Uncle Sandy came and took us to a farm just outside of Edmonton where my father couldn't find us.

Early the next afternoon, my uncle phoned Mom and told her to get someone to drive us by the backyard of our house. When we did, we saw my father screaming and cursing and throwing Mom's Bible and Spirit of Prophecy books into a fire. But after several days, he calmed down, and we returned home.

Although my mother loved my dad and attempted to meet his needs, the two of them became increasingly alienated, and my father seemed to sink deeper and deeper into the abyss of alcoholism. Then came an event that burned deep into me. Dad became so angry that he pushed Mom backwards down the basement stairs. I'll never be able to erase from my memory Mom's sad and horrified cry, "Oh, Daniel!" or the sound of her body crashing down those stairs.

Miraculously, Mom survived the fall with only bruises, though there were many of them. And the next Sabbath, undeterred by the events of that week, she took her place at the front of the church as the senior Sabbath School superintendent. She had given her life to God, and His church had become her world.

While my mother moved on from the abuse of that evening, I didn't. A brew of hatred began to grow in my soul, and I determined that one day I would step into the pushing, the cursing, the insulting, and the hitting and get even with my father. I intended to murder him.

I endured the strains and battles for several more years—and then came the fateful summer of 1963. That summer it all came to a boil. Two of my friends committed suicide. One rode his motorcycle down the main street of our city directly into the back of a parked truck, and the other went into the garage of his family's home, started the car, and sat on the floor behind the exhaust pipe.

Then late one afternoon, my father hit my mother again. That time I saw him do it, and, with a curse, I challenged him. He turned on me in shock and rage, but I was quick enough to get away from him and out of the house. He followed me angrily as I taunted him, yelling that he was too fat and too old to catch me. And then, just before I ran out of his sight, I made a threat that I meant with all my heart. I said, "If you ever hit my mother again, I will kill you. I will bide my time, but I will hunt you down like a dog and kill you."

At this, my father started to laugh. Because he was oriented to violence—once, he'd beaten his father so badly that he had spent two weeks in the hospital—he concluded that my challenge was a good sign, a sign that I was growing up. In a twisted way, he was actually proud of me. So, he cursed me and said, "I really think you mean it!"

I did.

After that incident, my friends and I took up activities that are a sure sign of troubled youth. We started to break into homes and take things. But we weren't after money or other valuables—we were after alcohol. We were well aware that virtually everyone in our neighborhood had a healthy stock of booze, so we considered every home fair game. When we couldn't get what we wanted from the homes we knew, we broke into the homes of strangers.

We followed a fairly simple game plan. In those days, most people didn't lock their homes even when they were leaving for a while, so we would just watch the target home long enough to ensure that no one was there and then walk in for the prize. When we had collected enough liquor, we would go to some vacant lot or schoolyard and "chugalug" it down—that is, we poured all of the alcohol into a jar and then took turns trying to drink the most of the brew. It was dangerous and stupid.

It was when I was in the midst of this stage that I began to come to my senses. I went to my mother during what I now call my two weeks of sanity and said, "Mom, if I don't go to a Christian school, I won't be a Christian." The simple truth was that I felt myself slipping away from a God whom I then knew only vaguely, and from the church that I cared very little for—and from my mother's love. I was in deep trouble and on the verge of even deeper trouble.

Something else had happened that added to my pain that summer.

Though I was far too immature to know in clinical terms what was happening to me, the fact is that I was shattered emotionally. I was broken. And even though I was only fourteen years old, I knew something was very wrong inside of me. I hungered for something. Just what that something was I didn't know.

In hindsight, I believe that the all-sufficient Jesus saw my need and sent the Holy Spirit to speak to me. He can tell even a fourteen-year-old kid in trouble, "This is the way; walk in it" (Isaiah 30:21).

So, I went to my mother, and she responded in a dramatic way.

Questions for Reflection and Discussion

1.   We go through this life only once. Consequently, in a spiritually divided marriage, the unbeliever is spending his or her life with someone who has different values, hopes, and dreams. What responsibilities do Christians have when married to unbelieving spouses? Should Christians give half of their time, energy, finances, and lifestyle to Christ and half to the unbelieving spouse? Seventy-thirty? Ninety-ten?

2.   What behavior on the part of a person justifies a Christian spouse's separating from him or her: Physical abuse? Psychological abuse? Spiritual abuse?

3.   What circumstances justify Christian parents' separating from unbelieving spouses to protect their children's spiritual lives?

Chapter 3

A Hand Moving in Unexpected Ways

My mother's voice woke me. What she said was stark but real: "Get up, and pack your things in this suitcase. We're leaving."

Mom had asked my father if I could attend the Adventist academy, and he had said, "It will never happen!" So she had made some executive decisions. She had arranged a job for herself several hundred miles away, on Vancouver Island, and she had called the business office at Canadian Union College and made arrangements for me there. She had also arranged for a safehouse where we could hide from my father until the school year began. Having made these arrangements, she then carried out her plan, and it all happened just about as fast as it takes to tell it.

Life changed. Our entire family would never be together again. My sister Mary stayed on with my father for some time, while Mom and I were gone.

Life changed in other ways too. Almost instantly the whole focus was different. Within two weeks of leaving home, I was taken to Lacombe, Alberta, and enrolled in high school at

Canadian Union College. I was open to a new way of life, and that new way came in spades: dorm worships, chapel assemblies, worship services with fellow students, and doctors visiting the campus and talking to the young men about taking cold showers. (Who had ever heard of such a thing?) These were all new experiences, and for the most part, they drew me into a closer friendship with God.

While my life was changing rapidly, some habits do die hard. Though I was just a fourteen-year-old, I was addicted to cigarettes. If I was to remain at that school, I had to stop smoking or go underground. The habit ended abruptly one day when I found myself blowing smoke into a paper bag while hanging my head out of my dorm window. Suddenly, and correctly, I had realized that not only did what I was doing *look* stupid—it *was* stupid. Definitely not cool!

Three things gave me stability and encouragement: my mother's letters, her food parcels, and her prayers. Over and over again, she reminded me that she had taken me to the college to put me in God's hands. She told me of her dream that I would be God's man, and reminded me that she had dedicated me to God. Unfortunately, the thought, though comforting, held little significance to me at the time.

Occasionally, I would return to Edmonton. There, my sister Nan, who was patient and kind, tried to give me guidance. Through those years, I was still trying to find out who I was and where I fit in.

I lived at Canadian Union College through eight often turbulent years—the years during which I grew up. Not only was that institution a school, it was also a temporary home and a place of refuge. There the dedicated Christian men and women who made up the faculty and staff provided me with nurture and support.

Of course, I didn't always think being there was all that wonderful. Counting beans in a confined space because of being insolent to a faculty member really didn't do much for me except hone my ability to distinguish between wheat, beans, oats, and barley. (Many years later, one of our publishing houses produced a book titled *Oats, Peas, Beans, and Barley*. That title gave me a good laugh!)

Being suspended from campus activities because I patronized a movie theater made me very uncomfortable. I still remember the principal dialing my mother's phone number and then handing the phone to me so I could tell her about my impending punishment. The disappointment obvious in her voice made me feel horrible. Now, when I look back, I can see how the hand of God was guiding faculty and staff members as they patiently brought me through my adolescent years in a way that didn't damage my body, mind, or spirit.

In the fall of 1964, during a Week of Prayer being conducted by Elder E. L. Minchen, I accepted the invitation to be baptized. I remember very clearly the day I experienced that special rite. I rejoiced over God's goodness and over the presence of my mother and my sister Mary.

Was Jesus sufficient to bring me through that period of my life? Of course He was. The patient and compassionate Savior was working in my life.

But while I had become a member of the church, I still had not fully found the grace of the Gracious One. I often thought of my family, of my home, and of my father, and the thoughts still made me angry, which I demonstrated often. Even though I was now a member of the church and sang in a quartet and in the choir, I needed more of Jesus in my life. Though I loved the music—the harmonies and the words—I knew little of the all-sufficient Savior.

When I graduated from high school, I immediately entered college, hoping to get a degree in economics in order to eventually enter the field of politics. Though I enjoyed the courses, something was missing. A thought had begun to work in my mind. It seemed to me that God was trying to speak to me. I was thankful for what had begun to take shape in my life, but I began to believe that the God who had brought me to this point now wanted something more of me.

Questions for Reflection and Discussion

1. Can you imagine leaving a home where one's belief in God was a major cause of anger and abuse and moving into a place that was basically supportive of one's relationship with God? What would that do for one's spiritual life? What unexpected spiritual challenges might it bring?

2. Have you ever seen Jesus working in the life of a young person who seemed to be an unlikely prospect for God's kingdom? What could more experienced Christians do to help such young people?

3. In a sense, baptism washes away our sins. Does it also wash away the scars that sin has given us? Does this happen instantaneously or over a long period? Can we do anything to hasten the process?

Chapter 4

Of Love and Ministry

I was eighteen years old when I entered college. I had become convinced that the business world was where I belonged, and for a short time, I actually flirted with the idea of becoming an accountant. I had scored high in that area on my aptitude test, so I thought I would explore the idea.

In order to test all of the possibilities, I made an appointment with an accounting firm to visit their office. When I walked in and saw all of the people sitting silently at their desks, I fled the scene without even having introduced myself. I was in sheer dread of living the rest of my life in a stationary position.

To this very day, I hold absolutely no disdain for that honorable profession. In fact, I stand in awe of those who practice it. I admire their faithfulness to duty and to the exactness of their profession. I simply praise God that He didn't ask me to do that kind of work!

During this period, something else came into my life and changed it forever. As strange as it may seem to those of us who are now chronologically advanced, an eighteen-year-old can

decipher genuine quality and grace. I discovered that Donna
Turner possessed all the qualities that a man could live with and
love for the rest of his life. I was not only attracted to her phys-
ically, but her spiritual commitment and her way of thinking
also drew me to her like a magnet. For the first time in my life,
I began to think about love and marriage.

I pursued Donna with a vengeance. I began to pray to
God, asking that He help me. But I was a child of the '60s and
focused on '60s music, while Donna was a pianist who was
deeply involved with classical music. It seemed to me that her
practicing occupied so much of her time that there was little of
it left for us to spend together. I remember complaining to the
women's dean that I thought Donna was married to the piano.

Driven by my overwhelming desire to be with Donna and
win her affections, I actually asked permission to sit in the
confined space of a music practice room and listen to her
practice! Not only was it agony at first to listen to the music,
but it was also agony because I couldn't talk to Donna. Of
course, one of the unintended consequences of this whole
process is that I gained an appreciation for classical music.

Yet while I was close to Donna in those hours I spent sitting beside a piano, the fact is that I was far from the spiritual
person she was. One day my roommate came into our room
and said, "Jackson, if you are ever going to convince that girl
to be yours, you are going to have to really change!" I knew
he was right.

While I thought the pursuit of this new relationship was
wonderful, the faculty and staff at Canadian Union College
were not so sure. I'll never forget being approached by one

faculty member, who rather ominously warned me that if I "hurt that girl," he would see to it that I "would never see the inside of the college for the rest of my life."

In the early days of our relationship, Donna gently led me into one discussion after another on spiritual things. Over and over again, she gave witness to the love of God for the human family. Though she often spoke of her love for her mother, she always defaulted to her love and dependence on her heavenly Father. Gradually, she led me to Jesus, and I began to relate to Him as my Friend. I also came to appreciate the love of a different kind of father than I had known—a heavenly One. The simple fact is that the All-Sufficient One brought a wonderful, godly woman into my life. She was and is the love of my life. Oh how grateful I am that Jesus knew exactly what and who I needed for a life mate.

We planned to be married in August of 1968 and worked through every possible hoop, including parental and legal permission, to be married as teenagers. All things being under control, we worked toward the date of August 4.

There was one significant problem as I looked toward our marriage—I didn't own a car, and I didn't have a driver's license. That problem was remedied when a man living in the college community offered to sell me his car. I bought it: a big 1958 Mercury Monarch with a push-button automatic transmission. Subsequently, I became very familiar with all of the farm trails and back roads of central Alberta as I prepared for the driver's exam. Fortunately, I passed the test the first time I took it.

Shortly after my purchase of a car and my acquisition of

a driver's license, I headed across the mountains to British Columbia to fetch my bride. Young people feel invincible. Their strength and energy often tempts them to take unwarranted risks. I was no exception. I started across those mountains with great anticipation. However, I wasn't thinking of just how tired I was when I began the trip. Well up into the mountains, about six miles east of a place called Chase, British Columbia, I fell asleep. When I did, the car careened across the lane of oncoming vehicles, flipped over, and landed at the bottom of an eight-foot-deep ditch. My two passengers and I scampered out of the car to safety, and we all thanked God for deliverance.

When the police arrived to investigate, the shape the car was in made them expect there to be fatalities. They took my two traveling companions to the hospital, and one of them remained there for several days. Me, they took to jail. I was held there for thirteen hours, until the circuit judge could come and examine my case. At the end of the day, he charged me with lack of the proper care and attention and fined me forty dollars.

Having gone through the trauma of the accident and feeling stressed because I was responsible for the serious injury a good friend had suffered, I spent the hours I was held in that jail asking question after question of myself. While I felt like a fool, I also started to consider another thought—that I'd been preserved from death for a purpose. Perhaps there was more to life than economics and politics. Perhaps the growing sense of being called to something much larger than I could have conceived was beginning to mature. In that jail cell, I determined that I would enter the ministry. I accepted God's call.

For the more than forty years since then, I've had the privilege of working for my all-sufficient Friend. I could never have weathered the joys, challenges, defeats, and victories of ministry without the certainty that I'd been invited to that position. It has brought me to places and privileges that I would never have dreamed of, and through it all, the Gracious One has brought me to the "high places of the earth" and into closer friendship with Him than I deserve. Yes, Jesus is sufficient—He is more than enough!

The basic fact is this: God's love for the human family took on a human expression. His name is Jesus. His care for us doesn't stop. He is, after all, the "Alpha and the Omega," the Beginning and the End (Revelation 1:8).

Life is an adventure. I can't think of it in any other way. While we often develop plans and attempt to chart our own courses, the steady hand of God moves us along when we let Him. And through the circumstances of life, we learn and relearn the great lessons of His love.

Questions for Reflection and Discussion

1. Who has had the most positive influence on you? In what way? Have you said thanks?

2. When have you been most aware of God's leading in your life? What made you believe He was guiding you?

3. The author says his life has been an adventure. Is that a good thing? Can everyone expect their lives to be adventures? What role does God play in this, and what's up to us? What could you do to make your life more of an adventure? Where's the line between adventure and presumption?

Chapter 5

Running With the Horses

"I f you have raced with men on foot and they have worn you out, how can you compete with horses? If you stumble in safe country, how will you manage in the thickets by the Jordan?" (Jeremiah 12:5).

These words recorded in Jeremiah's book of experience contain God's response to Jeremiah's state of discouragement. Called to be a prophet of God, he had decided to quit. Standing alone in the face of great opposition isn't easy, yet God did see the prophet through the darkest of times.

For me, settling into the ministry was a battle and a march. While I have never questioned God's claim on my life nor His call for me to enter ministry, I did wrestle with Him over issues that plague the church. So much was this the case in my early ministerial adventures that I have often described my first year in the ministry as three hundred sixty-five attempts to leave the ministry.

The patient saints in my first congregation must have pulled their hair out while I pastored there. Not only did I know precious little about being a pastor, it is also shamefully true that I didn't know how to preach the gospel. Oh yes, I was ready to win the world, but I couldn't preach Christ. The problem was that even though I was a pastor, I wasn't fully converted yet.

Discouragement and avoidance of problems marked some of those early years. The fact is that becoming a pastor in your heart and soul is, in reality, a huge collaborative effort that draws upon the pastor, the spouse, the family, and most importantly, upon God. The support my wife has given me during my forty-two years of ministry has been tremendous. Our three great children, Dena, Lara, and Danny, haven't always appreciated every facet of the ministry, but they have been constant in their support. They were genuine troopers even when we took them away from friends and dragged them halfway around the world. I don't say it glibly, but I say it again—the ministry has been a lifetime adventure for us.

But well beyond the faithfulness of my family is the loyalty of my heavenly Father, who just has not given up on me. What was true of the "weeping prophet" was also true of me. Yet with Jeremiah, I have come to understand that God's "compassions never fail, they are new every morning" (Lamentations 3:22, 23). His faithfulness goes well beyond the human ability to conceive words that could plumb its depth.

On the morning of November 30, 1980, I received a phone call that changed my life. The caller was from the General Conference Secretariat, and the subject of that phone call was an invitation to join the workforce of the Southern Asia Division. If we accepted the call, we would be stationed in Columbo, Sri Lanka, where I would serve as pastor of the Columbo English congregations and as the district leader of twenty-two congregations on the west coast of that little, teardrop-shaped island just off the southeast coast of India.

The battle that ensued in our minds was not small by any means. While Donna was very open to the call, remaining in Canada, where I was pastoring three congregations in the beautiful Okanagan Valley of British Columbia, appealed to me. I was enjoying my work, our children were enrolled in a great Adventist church school, we had just moved into a new home, and life was good.

I still remember thinking about the invitation and then quickly concluding that I would say No. I went to my home office and began to type a letter to the General Conference. I intended to preface it with expressions such as "Thank you," "I am honored," "God bless your search," and so forth. Then I planned to conclude the letter with the words, "I am turning down the call to Sri Lanka." However, before I could give it a final review, I had to leave to meet an appointment.

After several hours, I returned home and went to my office. To my surprise, I found a new and quite different letter lodged in the typewriter. It said, "I am so sorry that I cannot go to Sri Lanka. It would be very inconvenient for me in that I would not be able to find big green garbage bags in the supermarkets there." The letter went on at some length to express the hardship of accepting a call to a place that didn't have the conveniences of our homeland. My sweetheart was mocking me and trying to tell me through her humorous revisions of my letter that I should get serious about considering this call.

Jacob wasn't the only human being who wrestled with God. While I would never claim to have experienced the intimate, person-to-person battle royal that Jacob had, I did wrestle and agonize over that call. I kept praying repeatedly, "What do You really want from me, Lord?" And I kept expressing a verbal willingness to go anywhere He wanted me to. However, in my heart, I was hoping that going to Sri Lanka wasn't His will for us.

After two intensely challenging weeks, I discovered three principles that still guide what I do today. First, we mustn't draw a geographical circle that defines where we will and where we will not serve God. Second, we mustn't draw a circle of convenience around our service to God. And third, the safest place in the world for us to be is where God wants us to be. We concluded that God wanted us in Sri Lanka.

With those issues settled, I placed a phone call to the General Conference Secretariat in order to express our willingness to accept the call. To my shock and surprise, the response I got to my response was anything but what I expected. The woman on the other end of the phone line was consoling as she said, "Oh, I'm so sorry. We have just filled that call with someone else."

One might assume that a great cloud of disappointment settled upon me at that point, but just the opposite was true. I concluded that the call had only been a test and that I had passed the test. And I was absolutely delighted about what had happened. In fact, I was ecstatic. I ran to my car and went to find my wife. What followed when I found her was like the scene from the movies in which a man runs to his wife after they have been apart for a long time. I greeted Donna with the words, "It was a test. It was only a test! We don't have to go to Sri Lanka! They've given the call to someone else!"

I don't think that Donna was as happy as I was, but she still rejoiced with me. We hugged, and I said something that still haunts me today: "Now I can finish the basement!" In reality, the test had only just begun.

As we were eating supper that night, the phone rang, and the now-familiar voice on the other end of the line was cheerful and anything but consoling. "Are you still willing to go to Sri Lanka? The other individual has turned the call down." With a lump in my throat and with a few moments of reflection upon those principles of service that I had discovered, I responded by saying, "The reasons I gave you this morning still hold true tonight. Yes, we will go to Sri Lanka." I wanted to cry, but I knew in my heart that this was more than just a test—it was the invitation of God into a new world of experience that would again change our lives.

Leaving home and family does something to the human psyche. Even before leaving this continent, I felt lonely and insecure. Notwithstanding the convenience and swiftness of travel, it is somewhat daunting to pack up and move halfway around the earth. Everything is strange and different—the sights, the sounds, the smells, the language, the methods, the driving, and the eating are all challenging. Virtually nothing is the same. However, I had committed myself to going overseas for God. It certainly was not for my own comfort.

On the night of our arrival in Sri Lanka, I couldn't sleep. In my anxiety, I turned to Psalm 139: "Where can I go from your Spirit? Where can I flee from your presence? . . . If I rise on the wings of the dawn, if I settle on the far side of the sea, even there your hand will guide me" (verses 7, 9, 10). That beautiful statement of truth settled me down and gave me assurance.

There were times during our Sri Lanka experience when I felt like Jeremiah. I often felt overwhelmed. I wanted to quit, and at one point, I did turn in my resignation. However, God used Elder Rex Riches, my friend and president, to challenge me in a way I had never been challenged before. When I handed him my letter of resignation, he looked right at me and said, "You're a coward!" It was like a slap in the face, but I knew he was right.

I reversed my decision, and we stayed in Sri Lanka. Our experience there was not always pleasurable, but it was constantly beneficial. God was attempting to teach us lessons that would prepare us for the rest of our lives—and for eternity. In Sri Lanka, I realized that I had become satisfied with the status quo; that I had become accepting of my own complacency while condemning it in others.

Then we were called to India; there was a need at Spicer College. After some initial research and a visit to the campus, we decided to accept the call. Our family flourished there. I had the incredibly rich experience of teaching and pastoring on that campus. Donna went to school and studied under excellent teachers, ultimately earning a degree in English and religion. And our children loved it there.

I have often asked myself the question, What if I had followed through with my desire to quit while still in Sri Lanka? What privileges would I have missed? The sustaining Jesus kept hold of me during those wonderful and challenging days.

Faith is tested in the crucible of everyday experience. A faithful God stands with us as we allow Him to. I can only say that it was God who brought our family through that period of our lives. In the process, we have been extended privilege after privilege and blessing after blessing.

I have often thought of my life within the context of Jeremiah's statement, "This I call to mind and therefore I have hope: Because of the LORD's great love we are not consumed, for his compassions never fail. They are new every morning; great is your faithfulness. I say to myself, 'The LORD is my portion; therefore I will wait for him' " (Lamentations 3:21–24). Like Peter, who affirmed his Savior, often I want to cry out, "My Lord and my God!"

As that old evangelistic theme song says, "He's able, He's able, I know He's able. I know my Lord is able to carry me [and you] through." Dear friend, Jesus can take you through whatever you may be experiencing right now. And one never knows what will happen as we hold on tight to His hand.

Questions for Reflection and Discussion

1. Transitions can be hard on us even when God is leading. What can or should we do when we're beginning to feel we're on the wrong course?

2. How important is the support of our family to our success in the occupation we have entered? What can we do if our family isn't supportive or is even positively opposed to the course we believe God has led us to?

3. Can we—should we—expect to enjoy the work we're doing for the Lord? When should we stick it out, and when can we say we made the wrong choice and move on to something more compatible with our abilities and interests?

Chapter 6

Direction Enough

Being lost gives me some very uncomfortable feelings, including humiliation and frustration. It is commonly believed that if you are lost and can find the North Star or true north, you can find your path again. Of course, if you've forgotten whether you need to head east or west on the path, you're still in trouble!

My family's favorite instance of being lost happened in Paris, France. We had been home on furlough from our service in India, and we had decided that on our way back to that great land, we would spend some time touring through Europe.

We landed in Frankfurt and drove south to the Mediterranean. Then we headed for Paris to see the sights. We enjoyed our time in Paris, but after two or three days, Frankfurt drew us back. The trip back to Frankfurt seemed to be taking a long time, and I began to hear muffled laughter coming from the backseat. Dena, Lara, and Danny were chirping and muttering together about something, and I started becoming irritated. Finally, in exasperation, I blurted out, "What is so funny back there?"

Dena, our oldest girl daughter, responded, "Daddy, we have seen these buildings three times now!"

It was true. I had driven around Paris three times. Eventually, I got to the bottom of the trouble. The exit I was supposed to have taken out of the city had been blocked because of road-work, and I hadn't been able to find another route.

This experience, while humorous, is a very small shadow of what can happen to us spiritually without God's guidance. We often choose to set our sights on our own goals, needs, or predicaments, but seldom does that give us true satisfaction. New jobs, new cars, and new friends all bring a certain amount of joy, but they, too, do not suffice. The fact is that you and I have been created for another orientation—a spiritual one.

From the earliest chapters of Scripture and on, God repeatedly speaks about His willingness to give help and directions. To His people Israel, He said, "You yourselves have seen what I did to Egypt, and how I carried you on eagles' wings and brought you to myself" (Exodus 19:4). God's all-sufficient grace doesn't start and stop. It doesn't materialize and then vanish. The problem is that we do not sense it and take advantage of it.

Often, our ability to discern God's grace is greatly diminished by our desire to direct ourselves. This has been a sad feature of human experience. Hosea's experience illustrates all too amply the way things often are. "When Israel was a child, I loved him, and out of Egypt I called my son. But the more they were called, the more they went away from me. . . . It was I who taught Ephraim to walk, taking them by the arms; but they did not realize it was I who healed them. I led them with cords of human kindness, with ties of love. To them I was like one who lifts a little child to the cheek, and I bent down to feed them" (Hosea 11:1–4). God did all He could for Israel, but they turned away from His guidance.

Unfortunately, this response describes human experiences that have been repeated over and over again. Isaiah records God's description in these words: "The ox knows its master, the donkey its owner's manger, but Israel does not know, my people do not understand" (Isaiah 1:3). Through Jeremiah, God says the same thing in another way: "My people have committed two sins: They have forsaken me, the spring of living water, and have dug their own cisterns, broken cisterns that cannot hold water" (Jeremiah 2:13).

Yet the Bible gives us the assurance that while we may lose sight of God, He remains faithful to us. The prophet Jeremiah wrote these great words: "Because of the LORD's great love we are not consumed, for his compassions never fail. They are new every morning; great is your faithfulness" (Lamentations 3:22, 23).

For Christians, there is only one True North, and His name is Jesus. The Bible quotes Him as saying, " 'I, Jesus, have sent my angel to give you this testimony for the churches. I am the Root and the Offspring of David, and the bright Morning Star' " (Revelation 22:16). God anticipated the needs of the human family. Paul refers to this in his great statement: "What the law was powerless to do because it was weakened by the flesh, God did by sending his own Son" (Romans 8:3).

When we choose to look to Him, He can be found.

Whenever I've approached Him, and whatever the circumstances, He has been able to guide me. The reason this has been true is wrapped up in the promise of God Himself, who says to you and to me, " 'I know the plans I have for you, . . . plans to prosper you and not to harm you, plans to give you hope and a future. Then you will call on me and come and pray to me, and I will listen to you. You will seek me and find me when you seek me with all your heart. I will be found by you,' declares the LORD" (Jeremiah 29:11–14).

Though we may consider some of our requests for direction menial and small, He never sees them that way. The Word of God makes this very clear: "Do not be anxious about anything, but in every situation, by prayer and petition, with thanksgiving, present your requests to God. And the peace of God, which transcends all understanding, will guard your hearts and your minds in Christ Jesus" (Philippians 4:6, 7).

I'm going to repeat this text in another way, and then I'm going to list the parts that are particularly significant and relevant to you and me today—right at this point in our lives.

- "Do not be anxious about anything" (Don't worry about anything),
- "but in every situation" (like the one you're in right now),
- "by prayer and petition, with thanksgiving, present your requests to God" (by talking to God in the way that you do to your best friend).
- "And the peace of God" (knowing that God is fulfilling His Jeremiah 29 promise to you right now),

- "which transcends all understanding" (especially your ability to figure out the issues that are troubling you right now),
- "will guard your hearts and your minds in Christ Jesus" (God will watch over your mind and heart and will protect you because He has plans for you).

The following magnificent statement says it all:

Keep your wants, your joys, your sorrows, your cares, and your fears before God. You cannot burden Him; you cannot weary Him. He who numbers the hairs of your head is not indifferent to the wants of His children. "The Lord is very pitiful, and of tender mercy." James 5:11. His heart of love is touched by our sorrows and even by our utterances of them. Take to Him everything that perplexes the mind. Nothing is too great for Him to bear, for He holds up worlds, He rules over all the affairs of the universe. Nothing that in any way concerns our peace is too small for Him to notice. There is no chapter in our experience too dark for Him to read; there is no perplexity too difficult for Him to unravel. No calamity can befall the least of His children, no anxiety harass the soul, no joy cheer, no sincere prayer escape the lips, of which our heavenly Father is unobservant, or in which He takes no immediate interest. "He healeth the broken in heart, and bindeth up their wounds." Psalm 147:3. The relations between God and each soul are as distinct and full as though there were not another soul upon the earth to share His watchcare, not another soul for whom He gave His beloved Son.[1]

I have contemplated this passage hundreds of times. It brings security to me to realize that my life's direction—the way I live and the things I teach and believe—may all center on Him. He is the True North. He is the all-sufficient Guide.

Questions for Reflection and Discussion

1. Which of the many Scripture passages quoted in this chapter is your favorite? Why?
2. Have you ever seen a father enthusiastically praising his child for something that child has done? Can you picture God being as happy and proud of you and what you do? Why might a person find it difficult to picture God as happy and proud of him or her? What could enable that person to believe that God loves him or her just as extravagantly?
3. How could we share this picture of God with other people in such a way as to convince them that He feels that way about them? What do people do that makes this picture of God less believable? How can we get rid of the things that damage our witness?

Endnote

1. Ellen G. White, *Steps to Christ* (Washington, D.C.: Review and Herald® Publishing Association, 1956), 100.

Chapter 7

Manna and Grace: God's Provision

There are times when we discover the sufficiency of grace in the most unusual ways. The evidences are real, and the feeling is delicious. It shouldn't surprise us though. After all, our God is the God of the remarkable and the unusual.

I remember once when my conference president stood in front of us pastors with a face like a thundercloud. He was upset that his team hadn't produced the numbers that would have been acceptable to the brethren "upstairs." (It always seems like there is someone up there who needs to be pleased.) This president was a good man whom I deeply admired. I did not, however, agree with him on his approach at that moment. He thundered as he spoke. "You put a number on a piece of paper and hand it in, I want to know what you men are planning." With that he marched off the stage and disappeared.

Somehow, I felt compelled to "beard the lion in his den." I went after him, found him in the hall, and foolishly remarked, "Don't take this thing so seriously! There are still seven thousand

pastors who haven't 'bowed the knee to Baal.' " While that
broke the ice, he immediately asked me about the number I
had written down. My response—once again, rather foolish—
was "two million." He snorted a response. "Are you making
fun of me and the process?" to which I responded, "Are you
limiting the power of the Holy Spirit?" At that point things
broke down, and we both burst into laughter. I apologized for
my nonsense, and he apologized for being so intense.

Yet something compelled me to continue to speak to him.
I was struggling financially at that point and trying hard to
find ways to keep my two daughters in academy. As so many
know, the financial burden of providing Adventist Christian
education for one's children can be overwhelming. It had become like that for my wife and me. To be quite frank, it was
becoming a huge issue for us. Donna had actually gone log-
ging to provide funds for our kids' schooling. I watched her
get up at three and four o'clock in the morning and head up
into snow-covered mountains in order to provide the funds
we needed. We believed in Christian education then, and we
still do. We have no regrets.

At the end of the conversation with my president, he
looked at me with a strange smile and then said these beautiful words: "I have found a private donor who has given me
four thousand dollars for your children's education. He doesn't
want you ever to know who he is."

Tears welled up in my eyes as I thought of that. Someone
had provided me with a wonderful blessing—a gift with no
strings attached from a heart filled with goodness. Wow! That
was grace! The relief I felt at that moment was palpable. I kept

pinching myself because I was so blessed.

The children of Israel should have been pinching themselves on a regular basis as they contemplated what God had just done for them. A dry path through the sea, victory over their enemies, and the food they needed—all this should have been the stuff of amazement. The hand of God had set them free!

Unfortunately, though, by the time they arrived at Mount Horeb via the Red Sea, they were very unhappy. As a matter of fact, this story, recorded in Numbers 21, is one of the more painful stories of the Exodus.

The people were so angry that they openly complained about God and His leader, Moses. The Bible records their words to Moses: "Why have you brought us up out of Egypt to die in the wilderness? There is no bread! There is no water! And we detest this miserable food!" (verse 5).

The startling truth about their choice of words is that they were striking directly at the very instrument that God had chosen to use to bring about their deliverance. The manna was to sustain them throughout their entire journey, yet they looked at it with loathing and disdain. Somehow they had missed the fact that the manna was the instrument of God's grace. They were craving instead the flesh pots of Egypt. How twisted, when you think of it!

Suddenly, there were snakes, and then the people were facing real problems. Many were bitten, and some died. The people's troubles grew by the minute, and they called out to Moses, "We sinned when we spoke against the LORD and against you. Pray that the LORD will take the snakes away from us" (verse 7). And the all-powerful and all-sufficient God intervened again. God remedied the situation by making the serpent on the bronze pole the instrument of their salvation. As they looked up, they received healing and restoration.

Within the context of human ingratitude and rebellion, God laid out His master plan for taking care of the eternal needs of the human family. There He showed again the same provision that He had promised to Adam and Eve. He would provide the bread. He would provide Jesus, who said, "I am the bread of life. Your ancestors ate the manna in the wilderness, yet they died. But here is the bread that comes down from heaven, which anyone may eat and not die. I am the living bread that came down from heaven. Whoever eats this bread will live forever. This bread is my flesh, which I will give for the life of the world" (John 6:48–51).

The problem for the Israelites was that they didn't like the bread—they didn't like having to make the effort to go out and collect it every day. They didn't like having to eat it every day. They thought it strange that God couldn't just deliver it to their homes, so to speak. But the manna was a daily evidence of what God was doing for them.

Jesus saw the potential difficulty, and He told His followers and antagonists, "Unless you eat the flesh of the Son of Man and drink his blood, you have no life in you. Whoever eats my flesh and drinks my blood has eternal life, and I will raise them up at the last day. For my flesh is real food and my blood is real drink. . . . So the one who feeds on me will live because of me. This is the bread that came down from heaven. Your ancestors ate manna and died, but whoever feeds on this bread will live forever" (verses 53–59).

When we doubt the all-sufficiency of Jesus, we are just like those people. We have the same attitude. God has provided daily bread for us in the person of Jesus. Hebrews 7:25 makes this plain: "He is able to save completely those who come to God through him, because he always lives to intercede for them."

Every day He renews the offer of bread to you and me. How could we ever think that we can add to that?

Is that spiritual Bread sufficient to sustain us through eternity? Jesus says it is, and that's enough for me!

Questions for Reflection and Discussion

1. On their way to the Promised Land, the Israelites went through repeated cycles of up times and down times. What can we do to level those highs and lows and maintain a relatively stable relationship with God?

2. What does the Bible's picture of Jesus as the "bread of life" tell us about Him? About us?

3. Jesus said those who look to Him for salvation must eat His flesh and drink His blood. (See John 6:53–58.) From what Old Testament feast did He draw these symbols? What meaning did they take on after the cross?

Chapter 8

Good Enough to Break the News

I was getting ready for work the morning of September 11, 2001. That day the blue British Columbian sky enhanced the grandeur of the mountains. It looked like it was going to be a beautiful day.

The interruption came quickly and dramatically. The phone rang. It was our youngest daughter, and life was never to be the same. She was sobbing and speaking at the same time: "Turn on your television. They are flying jets into buildings in New York City." At first I thought she was talking about some science-fiction thriller, but she wasn't. We turned our television on just in time to watch the second jet hurtle into the second tower. My thoughts were, *We are at war! May God help us!*

Every news organization in the world wanted in on that story. A cacophony of voices from all over the world bombarded us for months. Those horrific images of celebration from the camp of Osama bin Laden were burned into our memories. It seemed like every day the news brought out some new sordid revelation of the cold, calculating, and horrible destruction of life in New York and of life as we had known it.

It became absurd. Everyone had a story, a tale to tell, some speculation to share. "Breaking news" logos were everywhere.

Isn't it amazing how people like to be the first to tell the news? And the juicier the story, the better. This is especially true if we are among the first to hear about it. It can become a matter of agony to keep from telling the news when we are asked to do so. Generally, we begin to let it slip out by telling only our closest associates. Then we widen the circle, and soon the story begins to come back to us, and so, since it's "out there" now, we don't hesitate to share it with everyone. Of course, the capstone to our arrogance in this matter comes when, on Monday morning, we can tell a would-be informant, "I heard that on Thursday!"

Have you ever thought about the fact that Jesus was the first to the share the good news not only of His victory but about you and me? We see that in Hebrews 6, which tells us about our all-sufficient Savior having this good news to share. In the first part of the chapter, Paul makes the argument that God affirmed His commitment to those who have faith in Him by swearing an oath so you and I can have continual and complete hope. Then, in his conclusion, Paul writes, "We have this hope as an anchor for the soul, firm and secure. It enters the inner sanctuary behind the curtain, where our forerunner, Jesus, has entered on our behalf. He has become a high priest forever, in the order of Melchizedek" (verses 19, 20).

The beautiful word picture that is painted here is priceless and unforgettable. The word *forerunner* used here is a word that, to the Greeks of Bible times, called up a wonderful picture. The forerunner was the one who shared the news of victory

with the waiting populace of a city involved in a skirmish
or war. Think of the amazing picture: The city is quiet, and
there is a sense of anticipation. Everyone is wondering what
is happening on the battlefront. Suddenly, a runner is spotted
waving his arms and shouting the news as he approaches the
city. "The army has won a resounding victory! We've won!
We've won!" And everywhere there is jubilation.

One day many years ago, my eldest daughter phoned me
and with exuberance in her voice announced, "I'm a five-star
girl, Daddy! I'm a five-star girl!" She had just been hired to
work as a masseuse in the spa of a very prestigious hotel. It
was a great victory for her. Believe me, I celebrated with her.

Now think for a moment of Jesus returning home to
heaven, having won the greatest battle ever fought. His victorious resurrection guarantees that Satan—His and our eternal
enemy—will not, cannot, ever return to power. The scene is
graphically portrayed in Psalm 24:7–10. David paints the picture. As Jesus and the angels come near the heavenly gates,
the angels chorus a demand: "Lift up your heads, you gates;
be lifted up, you ancient doors, that the King of glory may
come in." At this, an angel chorus inside the gates asks, "Who
is this King of glory?" The answer comes, "The LORD strong
and mighty, the LORD mighty in battle." Once again, the great
mandate rings out: "Lift up your heads, you gates; lift them
up, you ancient doors, that the King of glory may come in."
Again, the angels ask, "Who is he, this King of glory?" And the
chorus swells throughout heaven and the universe: "The LORD
Almighty—he is the King of glory."

Magnificent!

Jesus returned home to share the story of the greatest victory won on this earth! But He also brought other great news. It is humbling to think that Jesus would be described in Hebrews as your Forerunner and mine, but who am I to argue with the Bible? Our Forerunner has entered into the Most Holy Place of the entire universe to announce to His Father that you and I are on the way. Because He is able "to save [us] to the uttermost" (Hebrews 7:25, KJV), and because He is committed to interceding for us daily, He comes to His Father with the assurance that we are on the way—that, as Paul says in confidence, "he who began a good work in you will carry it on to completion until the day of Christ Jesus" (Philippians 1:6).

You see, when it comes right down to it, Jesus has already gained your victory! He puts it out there plainly when He says, "In this world you will have trouble. But take heart! I have overcome the world" (John 16:33). Paul says the same thing in a different way when he tells the Colossians that Jesus "disarmed the powers and authorities, he made a public spectacle of them, triumphing over them by the cross" (Colossians 2:15). Listen to him celebrate this thought: "Christ's love compels us, because we are convinced that one died for all, and therefore all died. And he died for all, that those who live should live no longer for themselves but for him who died for them and was raised again" (2 Corinthians 5:14, 15).

Can you imagine it? Jesus entering into the presence of His Father and telling Him with joy and jubilation, "They're coming! They're coming! Those for whom I shed My blood and who have accepted Me are coming! They are coming home

to heaven to spend all eternity with You and Me! Hallelujah!"
Well, that is exactly what the Bible says.

And you know what comes next: Jesus, as the Lord
Almighty, the King of glory is sufficient to say it and to do it.

Praise God!

Questions for Reflection and Discussion

1.   The word *gospel* means "good news." What makes the story
     of God and the cross good news?

2.   Do you consider the message of the Bible to be good news?
     When you tell other people about it, do they react as if they're
     hearing good news? If not, how could you make your witness
     sound more like good news?

3.   As this chapter points out, Scripture says, "He who began a
     good work in you will carry it on to completion until the day of
     Christ Jesus" (Philippians 1:6). What do you feel when you see
     an assurance, a promise, like this? Does it say anything to you
     about Jesus' sufficiency?

Chapter 9

Enough Without Me!

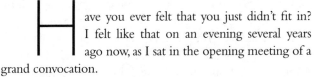ave you ever felt that you just didn't fit in? I felt like that on an evening several years ago now, as I sat in the opening meeting of a grand convocation.

I have experienced that kind of meeting as far back as I can remember. My mother always took me to camp meeting, and until she judged me old enough to decide for myself, she wouldn't allow me to miss a meeting. So, for instance, when the Junior departments had an empty hour or two in their schedule, I was required to sit in the adult meetings, even though I had little understanding of the theological issues that, to Mother's delight, were being discussed.

However, on the occasion in question, despite my acquaintance with the format, I felt ill at ease and alienated. The keynote speaker was addressing God's plan for human redemption and how God would bring men and women to experience salvation through His witness. Early in his sermon, he made the point that in Scripture most things are verified by the presence of two or three witnesses. He went on to say that this was also true in God's plan. His main point was that Jesus was only one of God's witnesses—that Jesus, by Himself, "was not enough"! God, he said, was waiting for the perfection of His people as the second great witness to His goodness and His plan.

I will have to admit that at that point I felt disconnected. How could what he was saying be true in the face of the plain statements of Scripture that proclaim the all-sufficiency of Jesus? For instance, Philippians 2:9–11 says, "God exalted him to the highest place and gave him the name that is above every name, that at the name of Jesus every knee should bow, in heaven and on earth and under the earth, and every tongue acknowledge that Jesus Christ is Lord, to the glory of God the Father." Jesus glorifies God in a way that no mere human can.

This point stands out in even greater clarity in what Paul wrote to the members of the church of Colossae. He says that Jesus "is the image of the invisible God, the firstborn [the causative agent] over all creation. For in him all things were created: things in heaven and on earth, visible and invisible, whether thrones or powers or rulers or authorities; all things have been created through him and for him. He is before all things, and in him all things hold together. And he is the head of the body, the church; he is the beginning and the firstborn from the dead [the most important One ever resurrected], so that in everything he might have the supremacy" (Colossians 1:15–18).

Though there are imitations, there aren't any second bests—nevermind equals.

It is true that God is looking for the revelation of His character in the lives of His people. However, there is no sense in which that revelation, whenever it comes, will ever compare with, be equal to, or add to the life witness of Jesus—either now or eternally. To say it simply: if God's character is seen in my life, then it is *God's* character, not mine, that is seen.

From the time I was a child, I have known the verses, "For it is by grace you have been saved, through faith—and this is not from yourselves, it is the gift of God—not by works, so that no one can boast" (Ephesians 2:8, 9). Paul goes on to say that "we are God's handiwork, created in Christ Jesus to do good works, which God prepared in advance for us to do" (verse 10). How can what is created ever equal the Creator? How can the clay be greater than the potter? How can the house be greater than the builder? If God's character is seen in me, then it is the result of an incredibly generous God who shares not only His love, but even His own character as well!

In the matter of God's plan for saving us, Jesus' life, death, and resurrection have demonstrated that His grace is full and complete. Ellen White has a great deal to say about sufficiency when she talks about how Jesus delivers grace to the repentant sinner. She makes it plain that His righteousness is required, and that when He gives it to us, there is nothing that we can add. For instance, she writes, "This robe [the righteousness Christ gives us], woven in the loom of heaven, has in it not one thread of human devising. Christ in His humanity wrought out a perfect character, and this character He offers to impart to us."[1]

I would never dispute the fact that we must mature as Christians through daily submission to God's leading and obedience to His will. If I have experienced His grace, then I respond by connecting my life to His. "When we submit ourselves to

Christ, the heart is united with His heart, the will is merged in His will, the mind becomes one with His mind, the thoughts are brought into captivity to Him; we live His life. *This is what it means to be clothed with the garment of His righteousness.*"[2]

As we live in the final days of human history, it is vital that we have a godly concern for our salvation. Paul counsels us to "work out your own salvation with fear and trembling" (Philippians 2:12). However, he doesn't counsel us to attempt to do this alone. He places the emphasis right where it belongs when he continues, "it is God who works in you to will and to act in order to fulfill his good purpose" (verse 13).

Scripture counsels us to take our role in our salvation seriously, but never within the context of attempting to add to what Jesus has already done for us. It is very clear on this matter, pointing unmistakably to the source of our spiritual journey. We are to "run with perseverance the race marked out for us, fixing our eyes on Jesus, the pioneer and perfecter of our faith. For the joy set before him he endured the cross, scorning its shame, and sat down at the right hand of the throne of God" (Hebrews 12:1, 2).

Even though we continue to struggle with the spiritual challenges we face, and while we need to have a God-oriented concern to be in Jesus and to have Jesus in us, these realities should never lead us to despair and hopelessness. We can rest in the assurance that since Jesus is the One who started the process, He will also finish it. Paul, writing to people he had brought to Christ, says he prays for them "with joy . . . being confident of this, that he who began a good work in you will carry it on to completion until the day of Christ Jesus" (Philippians 1:4, 6).

When it comes right down to it, we all have to face and answer the questions: Is Jesus enough? Can He take care of my needs? Is He big enough—powerful enough—to take care of the salvation of my soul and that of all the others who choose to follow Him? Are His life, death, and resurrection sufficient as a witness to me and to all other people that the God we worship is a generous and loving God? If not, then we have very little to say to our world.

Though I am called upon to witness to my loved ones and my world, there is nothing within me that gives me any standing with God. Whatever my abilities, they are not sufficient. I have no inherent spiritual capacity. Paul makes this very clear to the believers in Rome when he says, "What the law was powerless to do because it was weakened by the flesh, God did by sending his own Son in the likeness of sinful flesh to be a sin offering. And so he condemned sin in the flesh, in order that the righteous requirement of the law might be fully met in us, who do not live according to the flesh but according to the Spirit" (Romans 8:3, 4).

Let's abandon the idea that we can add to what God has accomplished through Jesus. And while it is God's ideal that we "become mature, attaining to the whole measure of the fullness of Christ" (Ephesians 4:13), it is not this that will ultimately satisfy the demands of the law or serve as an adequate witness to the world. Jesus, through His life, death, resurrection, and mediation for us, can Himself do that. But He who created the worlds is also creating a new person in each of us. And "if anyone is in Christ, the new creation has come: The old has gone, the new is here!" (2 Corinthians 5:17).

So your Lord and mine is committed to re-creating Himself in us. As we live our lives by His grace, we give witness to His love, His kindness, the truth about Him, His compassion—His grace. What a wonderful Savior! What a gracious Lord!

Jesus is the complete answer!

Questions for Reflection and Discussion

1. The author argues strongly that while God is seen in and through those who are converted, our witness doesn't in any way fill in for something lacking in the witness Jesus gave. What are the implications of the idea that Christians do provide something that Jesus couldn't or didn't?

2. What difference does it make to one's spiritual experience to see the reproduction of Christ's character in us as the continuation of His work for us rather than as the result of our efforts to meet Heaven's requirements—even if done only with His aid? Which better fits the name "good news"?

3. God wasn't dependent on preexistent matter when He created the universe. Might this truth offer insight to His re-creation of those who have turned their lives over to Him? What are the implications of 2 Corinthians 5:17? How can we best cooperate with Him as He works this in our lives?

Endnotes

1. Ellen G. White, *Christ's Object Lessons* (Mountain View, Calif.: Pacific Press® Publishing Association, 1941), 311.

2. Ibid., 312; italics added.

Chapter 10

Enough Power to Change

It was an exciting day. My father was coming to visit for what to us amounted to the first time. Many people take a father's visit for granted, but for us it was an event of major importance. He had been in our home only one time before, and that was when our eldest daughter was just a baby. He had never seen our two younger children.

He and his wife were supposed to come around noon, and we were ready for their arrival. But 1:00 P.M. rolled around, and there still was no sign of them. Somehow, my father had not taken down the correct directions, and unfortunately, this was well before the invention of the personal GPS.

My father managed to find our road, but he didn't know which house was ours. Then, just as he passed directly in front of our house, our son Danny ran out the front door and into the yard. When my father saw him in his rearview mirror, he blurted out to his wife, "That's where Danny lives because that's his son. He looks just like me!" Then he turned his car around and drove up the driveway to our home, and we had a great visit!

Genetics are amazing, aren't they? In the case of my son

and me, the old saying was true. The apple didn't fall very far
from the tree. It didn't take more than a backward glance for
my father to identify Danny. As a matter of fact, Danny still
looks somewhat like me, though he is much better looking
than I ever was. However, people can see me in my son.

In a place that we all are somewhat familiar with, but at
a time way off in the distant past, another Father came to
visit. Together with His Son and His Spirit, He made a grand
announcement: "Let us make mankind in our image, in our
likeness" (Genesis 1:26). Then They set about doing just that.

The Bible tells us that They accomplished Their task,
blessed the two They had made, and named them. The record
puts it simply: "When God created mankind, he made them
in the likeness of God. He created them male and female and
blessed them. And he named them 'Mankind' when they were
created" (Genesis 5:1, 2).

So the likeness of God was placed upon every human being by divine design. As a matter of fact, the original design
may still be seen in the human family. So, by faith we understand where we come from and whom we look like. We come
from God, and we are still identifiable as His children.

The apostle John, who describes himself as the disciple
"whom Jesus loved," gives a clear description of the relationship that our heavenly Father has designed and desired for
every one of us. "See what great love the Father has lavished
on us, that we should be called children of God! And that is
what we are! The reason the world does not know us is that it
did not know him. Dear friends, now we are children of God,
and what we will be has not yet been made known. But we

know that when Christ appears, . . . we shall see him as he is"
(1 John 3:1, 2).

This is true both of our physical selves and, even more
importantly, of our spiritual selves. God created us, and then,
though we were alienated from Him by sin, He adopted us
into His family again. Paul tells us that "he predestined us for
adoption to sonship through Jesus Christ, in accordance with
his pleasure and will" (Ephesians 1:5).

The exciting thought that jumps out at me when I review all of this is that from both the physical and the spiritual
perspective, we belong to God. We owe everything to Him
because He created us, and He is the One who can save us. We
belong to Him through both creation and redemption.

The all-powerful God does all of this through His Son
Jesus. Paul states this aptly to the Colossians: "In Christ all the
fullness of the Deity lives in bodily form, and in Christ you
have been brought to fullness" (Colossians 2:9, 10). Jesus has
sufficient power to create, and He has sufficient power to save.
It makes me want to shout for joy!

The reality becomes obvious when you contemplate the
answer to this question: If Jesus is powerful enough to create,
and if He is powerful enough to save, is His presence in my life
today sufficient to take me through any circumstance?

The answer that we must give resoundingly is this: Jesus
has more than adequate power to keep and sustain us. He
has said that when we entrust ourselves to His care, we are
in good shape. "My sheep listen to my voice; I know them,
and they follow me. I give them eternal life, and they shall
never perish; no one will snatch them out of my hand. My

Father, who has given them to me, is greater than all; no one can snatch them out of my Father's hand. I and the Father are one" (John 10:27–30). Jesus can take care of you and me in every situation.

Many years ago, my youngest daughter, Lara, brought me a totally discombobulated doll. It was one of those dolls that had been designed by the kind of person who would create a Rubik's Cube—the head, arms, and legs were all interconnected with rubber bands. Unfortunately, the doll my dear little girl brought me came in separate pieces: two arms, two legs, and a head—all of which had been disconnected from the body and from one another.

I tried to be calm as I asked, "Why did you do this to your dolly?"

Without blinking an eye, that precious little girl responded, "I did it, Daddy, because I knew you could fix it."

I assure you that, with that special incentive in mind, I spent the next several hours, tweezers in hand, repairing that doll. My determination to be worthy of my little girl's trust outweighed my clumsy fingers, my impatience, and my lack of experience with a doll like this, and by the next day I had made the doll whole.

Is Jesus wise enough, powerful enough, to pick up the fragments of a broken life? Can He move into our present situation and give direction, wisdom, and strength? Can He pull us back together?

Of course He can. And if an earthly parent will exert himself to repair an inanimate object, what is the infinite and omniscient Creator and Savior of humankind willing to do? Jesus answered that question directly: "If you, then, though you are evil, know how to give good gifts to your children, how much more will your Father in heaven give good gifts to those who ask him!" (Matthew 7:11).

Interestingly, when Dr. Luke recorded Jesus' words, he quoted Him as saying, " 'How much more will your Father in heaven give the Holy Spirit to those who ask him!' " (Luke 11:13).

Can Jesus restore His image in me? Of course He can—and will!

Questions for Reflection and Discussion

1. Do all human beings look a bit like God, or just those whom He has redeemed?

2. Which requires greater power: our creation or our redemption? What does this say about what we can contribute to either of these divine works?

3. God created us. And He has redeemed us, which means He paid the ransom for us. Does the fact that He made us and bought us make Him responsible for what we do? Why or why not? What does this say about our salvation?

Chapter 11

Sufficient Down Payments

I have purchased a number of homes. Of course, these transactions have occurred one at a time, and as is natural with the purchase of such a large item, I always wonder how well the investment will pay off.

Whatever the case, the process itself is pretty straightforward. If you are genuinely serious about the purchase of a particular house, then the first thing you do is to make a down payment. That generally is associated with a series of "subject to" clauses that protect the purchaser while demonstrating his or her serious intentions. Generally speaking, the greater the down payment, the more serious the offer of the purchaser.

In the summer of 2010, I was in Pugwash, Nova Scotia, at the camp meeting of the Maritime Conference, when I was called out of a meeting because of an urgent message from my wife. She had found a house in Laurel, Maryland, that she really wanted, so she was exceedingly anxious about the purchase. Our lives had changed quite dramatically that summer because we were moving to the Silver Spring, Maryland, area, where I would assume my new responsibilities with the North American Division of the Seventh-day Adventist

Church. If we wanted the house, we needed to make a down payment right away!

When it comes to homes, I always leave the style, the size, and the aesthetics of the home to my wife. My major concern is generally the garage—I like two-car garages. Nothing else really matters to me. So within moments of her request, I responded in the affirmative. She then faxed a copy of the down payment check to the realtor to demonstrate her good intentions.

However, more than good intentions were required. To purchase the house, she had to get on a flight from Toronto to Baltimore and show up at the realtor's office in Silver Spring with the real thing in hand in order to make the offer real. And that is what she did. She took off only a few hours after talking with me and made the offer good—made it sufficient. She went to great extremes to show the genuineness of her desire to purchase that house.

The Bible tells us that God has done that kind of thing for you and me. It is genuinely amazing! God has placed a deposit on you and me. "In Him you also trusted, after you heard the word of truth, the gospel of your salvation; in whom also, having believed, you were sealed with the Holy Spirit of promise, who is the guarantee of our inheritance until the redemption of the purchased possession, to the praise of His glory" (Ephesians 1:13, 14, NKJV).

Interestingly, the King James Version uses the word *earnest* instead of the word *guarantee*. The idea, however, is the same in both versions. The Holy Spirit serves as the promised guarantee—or earnest money, if you will—on God's purchase of the human family. We can live every day of our lives with the assurance that God has purchased us through the blood of Jesus. Every day we see evidences of the presence or prompting of the Holy Spirit, and when that happens, we need to remind ourselves that God is in earnest about our salvation. He demonstrated this through the gift of the Spirit.

Jesus made the promise, and the Spirit's presence in your life and mine today demonstrates that God is always as good as His word. "Nevertheless I tell you the truth. It is to your advantage that I go away; for if I do not go away, the Helper will not come to you; but if I depart, I will send Him to you. And when He has come, He will convict the world of sin, and of righteousness, and of judgment: of sin, because they do not believe in Me; of righteousness, because I go to My Father and you see Me no more; of judgment, because the ruler of this world is judged" (John 16:7–11, NKJV).

The Holy Spirit is present in our world today. All over this planet, men and women, old and young, come under conviction about their lives, their morality, and their accountability to God. You and I are among them. We are sinners even though we don't often like to admit it. Sin caused the death of the Son of God, so we cannot treat it lightly. However, even here there is a note of encouragement from God.

On our own, we can't differentiate between right and wrong. In other words, in our natural state, we default to rebellion against God. The Bible is very clear about this: "the carnal mind is enmity against God; for it is not subject to the law of God, nor indeed can be. So then, those who are in the flesh cannot please God" (Romans 8:7, 8, NKJV).

It is impossible, Paul says, for you and me to be naturally compliant with what God wants. So Jesus, in an act of eternal generosity, gave the Holy Spirit to the human family so that we can tell the difference between right and wrong.

Wow! The inference here is huge. Even when we sin and walk away from what God wants for us, He sends us a reminder, the Holy Spirit, to tell us that He is committed to living with us eternally. He is committed to the redemption of the purchased possession. In fact, God is so fixated on our redemption that He has lavished the greatest gift on us that He could give us. Read this part really carefully: "What then shall we say to these things? If God is for us, who can be against us? He who did not spare His own Son, but delivered Him up for us all, how shall He not with Him [that means with Jesus] also freely give us all things? Who shall bring a charge against God's elect? It is God who justifies. Who is he who condemns? It is Christ who died, and furthermore is also risen, who is even at the right hand of God, who also makes intercession for us" (verses 31–35, NKJV).

God gave us Jesus as an eternal expression of His love. Is Jesus truly sufficient? Does He make the whole picture fit together? Paul goes on to tell us that because of Jesus there is nothing that can separate us "from the love of God which is in Christ Jesus our Lord" (verse 39, NKJV). And it is the Helper, the One who stands beside us, the Comforter and Guide, who tells us with resounding clarity that Jesus is enough! In fact, "there is no other name under heaven given among men by which we must be saved" (Acts 4:12, NKJV).

As we enter into a friendship with Jesus, He just keeps on

giving. Paul tells this to the Colossians when he talks about how great Jesus is and how we find our own completeness in Him: "In Him dwells all the fullness of the Godhead bodily; and you are complete in Him, who is the head of all principality and power" (Colossians 2:9, 10).

What a down payment! What a Savior!

Questions for Reflection and Discussion

1. Scripture uses the image of earnest money being paid for our salvation. Who pays that earnest money, and what does earnest money guarantee? (See Ephesians 1:13, 14 in the King James Version.) What does this tell us about Christ's role and our role in our salvation?

2. What is the Holy Spirit doing in our world today? What is He doing especially for Christians—those who have already responded to God's call to them?

3. Colossians 2:9, 10 makes two important points: First, that the fullness of the Godhead dwells in Christ. Why would Paul write that to the Colossians—and to us? And second, he says that we are complete in Jesus. What does this tell us about our salvation?

PART TWO

OF HUMANS AND TREES

When we ponder the down payment that God has placed on the table of eternity for your salvation and mine, it is almost overwhelming. We rebel, and He loves. We rebel more, and He loves more! He doesn't give up. He commits Himself to a course of action and even reaction that is persistent, and if we will allow it, He floods us with an ocean of sufficient love.

We see the love of God illustrated in all His attempts to build eternal relationships with the human family. However, I now want to illustrate His love in terms of trees and the impact they have had on us all.

Trees! Scarcely do we recognize the role they play in our lives. They help us breathe, they shelter us from the wind, and they provide the material for the structures in which we live. There are few things better than sitting under a large tree in the summer and resting in its shadow. Poets have written about trees, singers have sung of them, and we cherish living among them.

Boys have a fascination with trees. When I was a boy, I was no exception. For several years, I went about climbing trees in order to enhance my collection of birds' eggs. However, after some time, I became bored with my egg collection, so my adventures into the trees for that purpose ended.

There was one tree that I never tired of—the tree in front of my boyhood home. It was a maple tree, thick, full, and round. I used to sit under it in the summer to get out of the sun. Yet my most vivid memories of the tree are linked also with the storms that roared through our city from time to time. I would sit under the tree during those storms and watch the lightning and listen to the thunder. I didn't realize how foolish that was; it was one of my favorite things to do.

I still enjoy thunder and lightning.

Joyce Kilmer penned these familiar words:

> I think that I shall never see
> A poem lovely as a tree.
> A tree whose hungry mouth is pressed
> Against the earth's sweet flowing breast;
> A tree that looks at God all day,
> And lifts her leafy arms to pray;
> A tree that may in Summer wear
> A nest of robins in her hair;
> Upon whose bosom snow has lain;
> Who intimately lives with rain.
> Poems are made by fools like me,
> But only God can make a tree.

God expresses His love to us through the trees. On page 10 of her book *Steps to Christ,* Ellen White made this comment:" 'God is love' is written upon every opening bud, upon every spire of springing grass. The lovely birds making the air vocal with their happy songs, the delicately tinted flowers in their perfection perfuming the air, the lofty trees of the forest with their rich foliage of living green—all testify to the tender, fatherly care of our God, and to His desire to make His children happy."

Three significant trees have shaped the experience of the human family.

Chapter 12

The Eden Tree and You and Me

The third chapter of Genesis chronicles the decision made by Adam and Eve that led to their exclusion from the garden of God. It was not just that they would have to move house and home as a result of their foolishness. Their decision genuinely reflected their own self-dependence and their lack of faith in the God who had created them. These are the painful words: "The man and his wife heard the sound of the LORD God as he was walking in the garden in the cool of the day, and they hid from the LORD God among the trees of the garden" (Genesis 3:8).

They were hiding among the trees in the Garden, but this event had its roots under another tree. It was the noblest tree ever to have graced this planet—full of beauty and symmetry, and vested with all the productive energy that only omniscience and creative genius can engender. Imagine standing under its lush and loaded branches. Its fruit was beautiful and inviting.

From a historical perspective, the tree of the knowledge of good and evil offered a tantalizing enticement: a power so great that it could change all that God had made through His creative act. It offered a power that, used in the wrong way, could bring untold misery to the human family. The greatest power ever extended to the human family was right there—the power to choose. *The garden of God was a place of choice—the ultimate in an eternal God's expression of the value of freedom!*

Think of Eve and Adam. Can you imagine them each standing in the midst of that lush foliage that only God Himself could have made? And as they stood there, they each faced a choice: Would they obey God, or would they obey the deceiver?

They could have chosen to rely on their own ingenuity and strength, or they could have chosen to place themselves under the protective care of God. They could have called upon God, and He would have been at their side instantly. But they chose not to. We make the same choice when we reject God's help. But we don't have to do that either.

Reflect on this magnificent statement from the book *Thoughts From the Mount of Blessing,* a statement that gives us insight as to how we may resist the deceiver: "He who is imbued with the Spirit of Christ abides in Christ. The blow that is aimed at him falls upon the Saviour, who surrounds him with His presence. Whatever comes to him comes from Christ. He has no need to resist evil, for Christ is his defense. Nothing can touch him except by our Lord's permission, and 'all things' that are permitted 'work together for good to them that love God.' "[1]

Adam and Eve could not have completely understood the extent of the consequences their caving in to temptation that day would bring to the human family. However, you and I have become all too familiar with those consequences. We witness and we experience the flood of bitterness that has come to humanity because of sin. We know that all the anguish, sorrow, and dying are rooted in Adam's mistrust of God's word—in his rejection of humankind's relationship to God. By nature we have become heirs of that bitterness.

They call the place Dutch Bar. It's a small settlement on the outskirts of Batticaloa, Sri Lanka. In the midst of the fabulous beauty of that shoreline, multitudes were slaughtered. I went to that place a few years ago and spoke with a young man who had lost his wife and twenty-three other relatives there. The pain of the moment was palpable.

That place is a reflection of Paul's statement in Romans 5:12–19. Notice particularly the words of verse 12: "sin entered the world through one man, and death through sin, and in this way death came to all people, because all sinned."

Without the intervention of God, we would have remained bound to an endless round of seeking but never finding; of speaking but never hearing a response; of wandering in a wilderness of human invention but never finding a home, a place of refreshing. But God didn't abandon the human family at the Eden tree. He planned for something better—something beyond the erring humans' comprehension!

Questions for Reflection and Discussion

1. In the Garden of Eden, Adam and Eve faced a choice, and they chose to do the wrong thing. In doing so, they sowed the seed from which came all the evil that has been done since

then. What was the essence of their sin?

2.   How were Adam's and Eve's sins related to all the sin and pain that resulted?

3.   If God really knew how much pain would come from Adam and Eve's sin, why did He allow them to be tempted? What values were involved? Why are they so important? What danger does discussing this topic pose?

Endnote

1.   Ellen G. White, *Thoughts From the Mount of Blessing* (Mountain View, Calif.: Pacific Press®, 1956), 71.

Chapter 13

The Marah Predicament

There is a second tree. (This is a fantastic story!) It is a marvelous example of the principle of healing and redemption that is so much a part of what God is all about. Moses lays it out for us in Exodus 15:22–26.

So Moses brought Israel from the Red Sea; then they went out into the Wilderness of Shur. And they went three days in the wilderness and found no water. Now when they came to Marah, they could not drink the waters of Marah, for they were bitter. Therefore the name of it was called Marah. And the people complained against Moses, saying, "What shall we drink?" So he cried out to the LORD, and the LORD showed him a tree. When he cast it into the waters, the waters were made sweet.

There He made a statute and an ordinance for them, and there He tested them, and said, "If you diligently heed the voice of the LORD your God and do what is right in His sight, give ear to His commandments and keep all His statutes, I will put none of the diseases on you which I have brought on the Egyptians. For I am the LORD who heals you" (NKJV).

This is a story of divine intervention; a story of God bringing His people out of cruel bondage. The people of Israel had been held as slaves in Egypt for centuries, and now they are being led out of that land. At the time of their deliverance, God had demonstrated His power to them on many occasions. Before their amazed eyes, He had laid out His determination to give them their freedom. God was setting them free!

With delirious joy and exuberance they had raised the chorus of Moses' song: "I will sing to the LORD, for He has triumphed gloriously! The horse and its rider He has thrown into the sea! The LORD is my strength and song, and He has become my salvation; He is my God, and I will praise Him" (verses 1, 2, NKJV; many other verses of the song follow). With those beautiful words of gratitude still in their ears, and with the memory fresh in their minds of a parted sea and of dry ground where the sea had been, they make their way to freedom.

They are three days into their journey. Three days of being together under the direct leadership of God. Three days of being a renewed nation. Three days of freedom! Oh, how they must have cherished every moment!

But then things changed. The day was *hot*! Out on the sandy plain they came to a painful conclusion: they were fast running out of water and there was none in sight.

One person in the camp was aware that there was some water close by, but knowing that it was near didn't make him happy. In fact, it brought dread. He was hoping that the Lord would choose *not* to lead the people in that direction. But to his utter amazement, Moses saw the guiding cloud head right in that direction.

As the people neared the water, they must have been filled with great excitement and anticipation. However, their joy changed to anxiety and murmuring when they discovered that they had been led to a bitter spring.

Our anticipations and expectations of events and places aren't always met with the desired fulfillment. Sometimes moments that seem to hold great potential disappoint us.

My wife and I had great expectations of our visit to the Louvre in Paris. We thought that touring that place would not only fulfill our dreams of seeing some of the greatest artifacts and painting ever known, but would also enrich our children culturally.

As we walked through the museum, our mouths hung wide open. We could hardly believe what we were seeing. However, to our children, the tour was a total bust. Even the *Mona Lisa* became the object of a great deal of scorn and derision. They were definitely not pleased.

This conflict between parents and children reached its pinnacle on the front steps of the Louvre. I looked at my eldest daughter and declared, "How many children have the opportunity to see some of the greatest sights in the world?" She replied in a rather direct way: "Dad! How many kids get dragged around Europe by their parents?" End of discussion. It just didn't turn out to be what we thought it would—so we went looking for crepes!

At Marah, the people's expectation and anticipation of

cool, refreshing streams of water evaporated with the bitter waters of the spring. The Bible says that then "Moses cried out to the LORD" (verse 25, NKJV).

Moses expected God to say or do something helpful, but Scripture pictures His response in rather startling words: "and the LORD showed him a tree" (verse 25, NKJV). How would you feel about that kind of answer to your prayer if you were in Moses' position? I think many of us would have thrown up our hands and said, "You've got to be kidding! What does that tree have to do with this bitter water? What do You want me to do with the tree?" Yet, if you are a student of Scripture, you know that this is the type of response that God has given time after time.

Second Chronicles 20 tells what happened when the nation of Judah was about to be mutilated by three angry enemy nations. Under the leadership of King Jehoshaphat, God's people gather on the steps of the temple in Jerusalem to appeal to God for help. Jehoshaphat prayed, "We do not know what to do, but our eyes are on You." And in response, God tells His people to call the choir, and there on the plain outside of the city, a choir brings a great victory to the people of God. *Amazing!*

Second Kings 3 tells the story of an army caught in the desert because of their arrogance and rebellion. They are facing imminent death due to a lack of water. They appeal to God for help, and God tells them to get on their hands and knees and dig.

Digging in sand isn't really what I would call a progressive experience. But out in the hot desert, an army ready for battle digs, and there in the desert God answers their prayers and meets their need.

The story recorded in Matthew 14:13–21 tells of another major predicament: five thousand people at a camp meeting, and the cafeteria has no food. But a little lad does, and Jesus takes the insignificant loaves and fishes and transforms them into the sufficient.

How many trees has God shown you lately? And how many will He show you in the future?

This pattern is *not* uncommon in God's dealing with the human family! People facing terrible circumstances come asking—pleading—for help, and God responds with solutions that defy human logic and common sense! The simple fact that becomes obvious here is that when we aren't aided by God's Spirit, we don't see as God sees; we don't think as God thinks, and we don't plan as He plans!

A brother-in-law of mine once purchased an old, rather valuable antique oak table. It was the kind of antique that one dreams about finding but seldom does find. It was very old and very ornate, and it was going to require a lot of work to restore it to its original state. My brother-in-law had a plan, a timetable, and an expectation, but these never saw fruition— because one day his boys thought they would surprise their father and make that table look good themselves. They painted the table with black metallic auto paint. I need not spend a lot of time sharing the conclusion of this story!

When we look beyond our foolishly conceived and often childish solutions and enter into the realm of faith, we come face to face with a God who can take the smallest, simplest,

and weakest object and turn it into a mighty instrument of redemption. His ways are beyond our ways. His wisdom is beyond
our wisdom and comprehension. The apostle Paul expressed his
amazement this way: "Oh, the depth of the riches and of the
wisdom and knowledge of God! How unsearchable his judg-
ments, and his paths beyond tracing out!" (Romans 11:33).

How difficult this is for those of us who believe in our
sufficiency! We want to analyze, scrutinize, and even criticize
God until we shape Him into just the kind of predictable
God that we want Him to be! However, the reality is something else. That's why Isaiah asked, "With whom, then, will
you compare God? To what image will you liken him?" (Isaiah
40:18). And God says of Himself, "I am God, and there is none
like me!" (Isaiah 46:9).

Moses cried out to God, and God showed him a tree.
Quickly, he cuts it down and throws it into the waters, and the
waters became sweet! *Fantastic! Praise God!* The blessing was
beyond anything the people might have conceived.

Ellen White describes the attitudes that God's people in
ancient times were plagued with when they met difficult situations. "The children of Israel seemed to possess an evil heart
of unbelief. They were unwilling to endure hardships in the
wilderness. When they met with difficulties in the way, they
would regard them as impossibilities. Their confidence in God
would fail, and they could see nothing before them but death.
He was ready to be a present help to them, . . . but they seemed
unwilling to trust the Lord any farther than they could witness
before their eyes the continual evidences of His power."[1]

There is a tremendous lesson here that we need to grapple

with—something that we need to experience if we are ever to be healed. The tree at Marah is a symbol of the human predicament. Without the power of God, we are all destined to live life without hope. However, through His mighty power and wisdom, He moves into our situations in order to reverse our fortunes. What seems impossible to us becomes the point of intervention for the all-sufficient God!

Questions for Reflection and Discussion

1. It seems that God frequently allows people to experience dead ends or other major disappointments in life. Why might that be? Is it because the people have done something that displeases God, or does He have some positive purpose for doing so? Ellen White wrote that God leads people in a way that they would choose for themselves if they could see the beginning from the end. What does that mean to you?

2. Point out some of the other biblical stories in which God uses unusual means to meet people's needs. Have you ever experienced that yourself? What reasons might God have for doing that?

3. How can we learn to trust God so deeply that we don't worry or become upset when He chooses to step outside the normal ways to meet our needs? Why does He act this way so often? What does His methodology teach us?

Endnote

1. Ellen G. White, *Spiritual Gifts* (Washington, D.C.: Review and Herald®, 1944), 3:249, 250.

Chapter 14

God's Eternally Sufficient Solution Tree

All normal humans seek happiness. We all seek to find a way into a kind of Promised Land of our own expectations. So often in our attempts to discover our ideals and our philosophical and physical and intellectual sweet spots, we wind up finding bitterness. We make plans and then proceed to fulfill our dreams, but without God in the center of our lives, we feel an emptiness of soul. We feel a hunger for something more—for something that goes beyond our possessions and our experiences; for something that goes beyond the tangible. And we cast about attempting to find solutions to our dilemma: a new career, a new home, a new wife, a new "feel good" substance, a new drink, a new boyfriend, a new experience, a new counselor. For some, this search goes on for a lifetime.

We study and search for ways to correct the problem, to fill the void, to quench the thirst, but we come up empty; we come up dry every time! We construct all kinds of solutions, but all too often the streams we find are filled with bitter water! Why is that?

God Himself gives us the answer: "My people have committed two sins: They have forsaken me, the spring of living water, and have dug their own cisterns, broken cisterns that cannot hold water" (Jeremiah 2:13).

Human schemes and human wisdom seldom bring us happiness. We know ourselves too well. And everything human is too limited to allow us to picture Him adequately. So, our experience and knowledge of ourselves may sometimes bring us to despair, leading us in our hopelessness to cry out to God, "How are we to move beyond our current circumstances? How can we find the fresh streams? How can we see things as God sees them and not as we envision them?"

Paul instructs us: "Do not deceive yourselves. If any of you think you are wise by the standards of this age, you should become 'fools' so that you may become wise. For the wisdom of this world is foolishness in God's sight" (1 Corinthians 3:18, 19). And in a poignant statement, Ellen White gives us a clear picture of the human state and what God has to offer us: "It is impossible for us, of ourselves, to escape from the pit of sin in which we are sunken. Our hearts are evil, and we cannot change them. . . . Education, culture, the exercise of the will, human effort, all have their proper sphere, but here they are powerless. They may produce an outward correctness of behavior, but they cannot change the heart; they cannot purify the springs of life."[1]

So we try and fail, and try and fail. And in our exhaustion, we cry out, "Help us, God! Please help us!" *And He shows us a tree!*

Paul tells us about this tree when he says, "Christ has redeemed us from the curse of the law, having become a curse for us, (for it is written, 'Cursed is everyone who hangs on a tree')" (Galatians 3:13, NKJV). Peter informs us of the same truth: "[He] Himself bore our sins in His own body on the tree, that we, having died to sins, might live for righteousness—by whose stripes you were healed" (1 Peter 2:24, NKJV).

With this tree, the precious cross of Jesus, God gives us the opportunity to choose again. Thank God that He did not cut off grace or choice at the Eden tree. Thank God that Paul, under the inspiration of the Holy Ghost, went on in his statement in Romans 5 to say, "For if, by the trespasses of one man, death reigned through that one man, how much more will those who receive God's abundant provision of grace and of the gift of righteousness reign in life through the one man, Jesus Christ!" (verse 17).

At the Cross, we have the opportunity of looking into the face of God and saying, "I'll be Yours forever! Take me! Use me! I trust my life now and eternally with You!" God will respond to this commitment, saying, "I am the LORD who heals you" (Exodus 15:26, NKJV).

The cross is the tree that God threw into the ocean of human need. It reverses the bitterness of the person who stands alone without God. It is God's solution to our problems!

So, what am I to do with the tree—this precious gift from Calvary? Matthew records Jesus' answer: "He who does not take his cross and follow after Me is not worthy of Me. He who finds his life will lose it, and he who loses his life for My sake will find it" (Matthew 10:38, 39, NKJV). And Paul says, "The message of the cross is foolishness to those who are perishing, but to us who are being saved it is the power of God" (1 Corinthians 1:18).

So what am I to do with the tree? I am called upon to take the tree with me everywhere I go and through all that I experience. Into the pool of my despair I cast the tree. Into the slough of my pain I carry it. Into the oceans of my wild emotions I bring the tree. In times of temptation and failure and heartache and in times when I am over my head in the waters of uncertainty, I draw upon the soul-saving power of the tree. And in the moment of my joy, I hear the splash of the tree in the sweet waters of the soul!

We turn to the Bible to see what God would tell us: "It pleased the Father that in Him all the fullness should dwell, and by Him to reconcile all things to Himself, by Him, whether things on earth or things in heaven, having made peace through the blood of His cross" (Colossians 1:19, 20, NKJV).

Referring to the experience of the Christian with the cross, Paul says, "I have been crucified with Christ; it is no longer I who live, but Christ lives in me; and the life which I now live in the flesh I live by faith in the Son of God, who loved me and gave Himself for me" (Galatians 2:20, NKJV).

And, finally, he just comes right out and tells us that we have nothing to boast of in ourselves. "God forbid that I should boast except in the cross of our Lord Jesus Christ, by whom the world has been crucified to me, and I to the world" (Galatians 6:14, NKJV).

Ellen White comments on this perspective: "None are so sinful that they cannot find strength, purity, and righteousness in Jesus, who died for them. He is waiting to strip them of their garments stained and polluted with sin, and to put upon them the white robes of righteousness; He bids them live and not die."[2]

The Calvary tree provides hope for a world in need— hope for you and for me!

Many years ago, I was conducting a series of evangelistic meetings in Winnipeg, Canada. At the end of the presentation one evening, I invited the listeners to come to the front of the church as an indication that they were putting themselves in Jesus' hands. One woman who had been attending faithfully was among those who came forward. I was delighted but surprised: her family circumstances were such that she was almost certain to find persecution waiting for her if she revealed to her husband that she had made such a commitment.

When she came forward, she stood directly in front of me. Foolishly, I asked her if she wasn't risking her safety as a result of her decision. I will never forget the incredulous look on her face as she said to me, "Pastor, after all that Jesus has done for me, how can I do anything less for Him?" She was right.

The fact is that when we are faced with the realities of God's love for each of us, we come face to face with the realities of grace. God has done something for us well beyond the spectrum of human ability. It is beyond the highest thought that we can think. It is beyond our wisdom, our ingenuity, and our strength. He is all powerful, ever present, all knowing. His gift of Jesus to the human family is all sufficient. In other words, dear reader, *Jesus is enough*! "Behold!

The Lamb of God who takes away the sin of the world!"
(John 1:29, NKJV).

Questions for Reflection and Discussion

1. Is it wrong to look for a degree of pleasure and satisfaction in
    the things the author lists in the first paragraph of this chapter:
    things such as a career, a house that appeals to us, marriage,
    exciting vacations, and so forth? When does our enjoyment of
    these things become spiritually dangerous?
2. The author refers to Ellen White's description of our predicament
    in that we are sunk in a pit of sin that we can't escape because
    our hearts are evil. What does the "tree" highlighted in this
    chapter do that pulls us out of that pit?
3. Despite Adam and Eve's misuse of the freedom to choose,
    which God had given them, He didn't withdraw this great gift.
    How important is it today, and how can we use it in the right
    way?

Endnotes

1. Ellen G. White, *Steps to Christ*, 18.
2. Ibid., 53.

PART THREE

THE TRANSACTIONS OF GRACE

The Bible has a great deal to say about Jesus' ability to bring about the full and complete salvation of the human family. As a matter of fact, if we can't find this truth clearly in the Bible, we won't find it at all. We really have no other place else to go.

When we come face to face with the transactions of grace, we recognize the fact that as God planned for the eternal benefit and blessing of the eternal family, He had in mind that what He would accomplish through Jesus would be fully sufficient—all that was needed to supply all human need. John, the author of Revelation, tells us that Jesus was and is "the Lamb who was slain from the creation of the world" (Revelation 13:8). Through His life, death, and resurrection, we can see the transactions of grace.

Chapter 15

Transaction 1: God Stoops Down

Most of us dream. Often our dreams lead us to desire something. We wish we had _____. We wish we were _____. We wish we could _____. When I was a youngster going to school, I would sometimes exchange sandwiches with my schoolmates because their mother's peanut butter just had to taste better than the peanut butter my mother had spread on my sandwiches. And in moments of daydreaming and fantasy, it is not unusual for us to wonder what it would be like to change places with the rich and famous—even if it were for only a moment.

But think of this. If you have never experienced the danger of battle, the loneliness of imprisonment, the agony of torture, or the pangs of starvation, you are better off than the millions of people in the world who are all too familiar with these things. Would you willingly exchange your life for theirs? I don't think so!

However, in 2 Corinthians 5:21, we discover an exchange

of such an extreme magnitude that it fills us with wonder. It boggles our imaginations. It is higher than the highest human thought can reach. The Bible makes this amazing statement: "[God] made Him who knew no sin [that is, Jesus] to be sin for us, that we might become the righteousness of God in Him" (2 Corinthians 5:21, NKJV).

When you read this statement for the first time, it can seem very daunting and ethereal. However, when you take a closer look, you discover several wonderful thoughts. First, a great exchange took place in order to bring about harmony between God and humans. Second, the sinless Jesus was the center of this exchange. Third, because of the exchange, we receive the righteousness of Jesus through faith. God stoops low and enters into the human predicament. Jesus comes as a babe, grows into manhood, and exchanges all that He is for all that we are. Now that is a complete change!

Have you ever thought about what it would be like to be absolutely spotless—sinlessly clean? It's a difficult question because we have no frame of reference within which to answer it. Perhaps a newborn child is the closest thing we know to absolute innocence and purity. I remember as though it were yesterday holding our first child in my arms for the first time. While it was an experience of joy, it was also somewhat frightening. She was so tiny, so fragile, so dependent and vulnerable. I was actually afraid of dropping her.

Time, however, has an interesting way of bringing out the realities that lie behind the personality of every individual. It doesn't take very long till changes come. Till there is an angle. Till human nature as we know it now begins to emerge. Till people begin to manipulate circumstances. All of us do this in one way or another.

My wife and I were brought face to face with this reality one day as we were bringing our children—our two daughters at that time—home from shopping. Our daughters had been very good throughout the shopping trip, and we had rewarded them each with a big cookie.

From birth on, our oldest daughter had a great appetite. She summarily devoured everything that was placed before her. Not so our youngest daughter. She was pickier about what she ate. Our confrontation with reality that day started with a conversation between the two children that commenced after our oldest daughter had finished her cookie. "Lara," she said, "do you know what love is?" When there was no response from her cookie-nibbling sister, she went on as if commissioned to do so. "Love is sharing your cookie, and you haven't even given me one bite."

And so it goes. In general, we humans focus on ourselves. Only those whom the Spirit of God controls see primarily the wants and needs of other people.

However, focus on self was not a part of Jesus' character. That's why Dr. Luke could write about Jesus' early life and His development: "Jesus grew in wisdom and stature, and in favor with God and man" (Luke 2:52).

When you consider Jesus' miracles, when you consider the compassion with which He reached out to touch the bruised and broken men and women, then you know something of the magnitude of Dr. Luke's statement. Jesus constantly looked to others, seeking their good.

While the temptations of Jesus were very real, while He could have caved in and sinned, the fact is that He did not. He remained pure and noble. There was nothing in Him that would give rise to rebellion against God.

After Jesus' death, the recollections of His friends, those who had been closest to Him, bore out this truth. Peter said it so clearly: " 'He committed no sin, and no deceit was found in his mouth.' When they hurled their insults at him, he did not retaliate; when he suffered, he made no threats. Instead, he entrusted himself to him who judges justly" (1 Peter 2:22, 23). This is how Jesus—this holy, harmless, sinless Son of God and Son of man—became the center, the focus of the gracious exchange.

Why would He do that? Why would He even contemplate trading places?

The answer is this: It was a part of the plan of God for your eternal happiness and mine. Who else could have done it? Certainly not you or me.

Questions for Reflection and Discussion

1. The first part of this chapter pictures the great exchange. Can you think of anything—any event in history or in nature—that offers us insight into what Jesus did when He "became sin" for us (2 Corinthians 5:21)?

2. Did Jesus actually become sin for us, or is this a kind of spiritual exaggeration used to communicate how much He loves us?

3. What effect did Jesus' becoming sin for us have on Him? On sinners?

Chapter 16

Transaction 2: Jesus Becomes Like Us

P aul told the Corinthians, "God made Him who had no sin to be sin for us."

Hold on to your seats—this is horrible! Isn't it we who are supposed to become like Him? Why is it that He became like us?

Human nature isn't very pretty. Using the words *Jesus* and *sinner* in the same sentence just seems so wrong. However, that is what the Bible says here. How are we to understand it?

Generally, it isn't difficult for us to recognize that something is wrong—immoral. We know how to distinguish between guilt and innocence because Jesus has given us the precious gift of the Holy Spirit so we can recognize sin and "righteousness and judgment" to come (John 16:8). Without the Holy Spirit, we don't have this ability, for as Scripture says, "the mind governed by the flesh is hostile to God; it does not submit to God's law, nor can it do so" (Romans 8:7). So it shouldn't be difficult for us to understand the contrast that I will make with the following two stories.

During much of 1985, Los Angeles was terrorized by a series of sex killings. Thirteen women were raped, mutilated, and then murdered. By the summer of that year, there were forty-three incidents that the authorities had attributed to a vicious killer whom the police had nicknamed "the Night Stalker." The criminal's real name was Richard Ramirez. He was a confirmed Satanist; his actions clearly demonstrated this.

On the evening of August 31, 1985, Ramirez, who had left the city temporarily, returned. Then, to his horror, he discovered that the police had been able to identify him and had plastered posters of him throughout the city. Ramirez immediately decided to get out of town again.

In his desperation to leave, Ramirez decided to steal a car. But not just any car would do. He wanted a "muscle car"—a car with a big engine. He found one, but the owner of the vehicle was underneath it, working on it. Ramirez tried to take it anyway. But when he tried to start the car, the owner scrambled out from underneath it. When he saw Ramirez, he recognized him as the man on the posters, so he started hollering at the top of his lungs, "The Night Stalker! The Night Stalker!"

Startled neighbors heard the cry and came out of their houses to see this notorious villain. Within minutes, a very large crowd had gathered, and they began to chase Ramirez. He ran for his life, but eventually, the crowd surrounded him. They would have killed him on the spot if it hadn't been for the arrival of the police.

So, the Night Stalker was captured and justice was done to this guilty sinner.

Now for the other story about a condemned criminal and

a crowd—one in which things get twisted and become bizarre. This time, the mob—an enraged crowd of people, surrounds the courtroom of Pilate, the procurator of Judea, failing to recognize the obvious.

Let's observe the infamous proceedings there more closely. This crowd, enflamed by demons in human form, has cried out for blood. What had they seen? Why were they so angry?

As we view the scene in front of us, we see Pilate, the compromising procurator, with Jesus, the accused. But what a contrast! Pilate was always calculating, always contemplating his advancement—his upward mobility, his ascension into greatness.

Right beside him is Jesus, who taught and lived the truth that "unless a kernel of wheat falls to the ground and dies, it remains only a single seed. But if it dies, it produces many seeds" (John 12:24). In the gospel of Jesus, people aren't valued for their upward mobility; His followers don't ascend into greatness; rather, they descend into greatness! That greatness is found when they are planted in the soil of human need.

As a matter of truth, Jesus' life, death, and resurrection are wonderful demonstrations of the principle that governs all of the activities of heaven. Ellen White says, "It will be seen that the glory shining in the face of Jesus is the glory of self-sacrificing love. In the light from Calvary it will be seen that the law of self-renouncing love is the law of life for earth and heaven; that the love which 'seeketh not her own' has its source in the heart of God."[1]

In the midst of all of this, Pilate finds what he believes to be a way out of the predicament in which he has found himself.

Warned by his wife to steer clear of Jesus, and certain that the prisoner is innocent, he attempts to extricate himself from the situation by announcing to the crowd that he will release a prisoner. It is just a phony way to placate the Jews with a false honoring of a Jewish custom.

Then Barabbas is introduced to the crowd. He's a seditious criminal, and he actually had the nerve to stand in front of the crowd and curse and threaten them. And Jesus is right there beside him—the Son of man, and the Son of God acting as a lamb before the slaughter, not speaking at all!

Think this through very carefully now! History and Scripture inform us bluntly that on this day the crowd called for the binding of the innocent and the release of the guilty. In more contemporary terms, we would say they released Osama bin Laden and crucified Jesus!

What is so shocking, so perversely shocking, when you carefully analyze this process and fully grasp the eternal consequences of the trial of Jesus, is that here, at the point of Jesus being condemned to death on a cross, we are directly exposed to the mind of God and to the way He thinks. Arriving at this conclusion is painful because it hurts our egos and it flies in the face of the way we think. But in reality, it comes down to this scene in an ancient courtroom in Jerusalem. Either Jesus is crucified and we are released, or we are crucified and Jesus is released. The Bible writers make this point very clearly: "Christ has redeemed us from the curse of the law, having become a curse for us (for it is written, 'Cursed is everyone who hangs on a tree')" (Galatians 3:13, NKJV). "[He] Himself bore our sins in His own body on the tree, that we, having died to sins, might live for righteousness—by whose stripes you were healed" (1 Peter 2:24, NKJV). "Christ's love compels us, because we are convinced that one died for all, and therefore all died" (2 Corinthians 5:14).

Ellen White also makes this clear. Notice these amazing statements: "The world's Redeemer gave himself for us. Who was he?—The Majesty of heaven, pouring out his blood upon the altar of justice for the sins of guilty man."[2] "God suffered His wrath against transgression to fall on His beloved Son. Jesus was to be crucified for the sins of men."[3] "He who stilled the angry waves and walked the foam-capped billows, who made devils tremble and disease flee, who opened blind eyes and called forth the dead to life,—offers Himself upon the cross as a sacrifice, and this from love to thee. He, the Sin Bearer, endures the wrath of divine justice, and for thy sake becomes sin itself."[4]

Just exactly what does God see as He views the Cross? Does He now see the pure and sinless Jesus? The One who spoke worlds into existence?

The painful answer we must give is No! A thousand times No!

Scripture informs us that while God does see Jesus at the time of the Crucifixion, He sees Him as the embodiment of your sins and mine! And it is a horrific sight! The Bible writers speak: "[He] Himself bore our sins in His own body on the tree" (1 Peter 2:24, NKJV). "We all, like sheep, have gone astray, each of us has turned to our own way; and the LORD has laid on him the iniquity of us all" (Isaiah 53:6).

God sees your sin and mine. It was this that caused Him

to turn away from His Son. It was this that caused Jesus anguish so that He cried out, "My God, my God, why have you forsaken me?" (Matthew 27:46). "Yet it was the LORD's will to crush him and cause him to suffer, and though the LORD makes his life an offering for sin, he will see his offspring and prolong his days, and the will of the LORD will prosper in his hand" (Isaiah 53:10).

Think of it: God made Him to be sin for us!

Questions for Reflection and Discussion

1. The author says it's easy for us to see why we should become like Jesus. The difficult question is why He had to become like us—like sinful human beings. Was He really like us, or was this only a figure of speech?

2. What must we have to be able to recognize sin? Why can't we recognize it without this aid?

3. What is it that the exchange featured in this chapter does for us spiritually? What role does it play in settling the great controversy that's been going on since Lucifer rebelled in heaven?

Endnotes

1. Ellen G. White, *Our Father Cares* (Hagerstown, Md.: Review and Herald®, 1991), 200.

2. White, *Review and Herald*, March 21, 1893.

3. White, *The Desire of Ages* (Mountain View, Calif.: Pacific Press®, 1940), 743.

4. Ibid., 755, 756.

Chapter 17

Transaction 3: We Become Like Him

During the time that our family spent in India, I had the privilege of teaching homiletics in the religion department at Spicer Memorial College. Every year as we would begin the class, I would give a brief introductory statement that went like this: While we are all to learn from one another, and while there is very little that is new under the sun, God has called you into the ministry so that His grace and His message can shine out through you. Please make certain that you do not cover over who you are with other preachers' styles or mannerisms.

Inevitably, my young preachers would stand up for their first presentation and an instant metamorphosis would take place. They would become living likenesses of the two "model preachers" who were working for the Southern Asia Division at that time: Pastor John Wilmott, the ministerial director of the division, and Dr. John Fowler, the director of education. Both of these men had unique styles and mannerisms, and both of them were powerful preachers. It took time and effort to teach my students that as great as those two men were, preachers needed to operate out of their own context and personality. They needed to allow the gospel to be seen through their uniqueness.

It is a human tendency to find a model that we admire and then to emulate that person or to adopt that way of thinking or acting. The last portion of 2 Corinthians 5:21 speaks of this from a spiritual perspective. I am thankful that the apostle Paul concluded his statement with these words: "that we might become the righteousness of God in Him" (NKJV).

Praise God that the process of the exchange didn't stop in the tomb. Jesus lives! God's victory over evil didn't end in the death of Jesus, because when God starts a job, He finishes it! In the resurrection of His Son, He forever obliterates the hold that the devil has over humankind—in both the physical and the spiritual realms.

If time lasts long enough, all of us will die. But, praise God, we won't stay dead. As much as we view and understand death as a negative, the fact is, according to Paul, that Jesus has conquered death! The sting of death and its permanence have been removed for those who accept the great exchange. The triumphant words of Paul give us this assurance:

> Listen, I tell you a mystery: We will not all sleep, but we will all be changed—in a flash, in the twinkling of an eye, at the last trumpet. For the trumpet will sound, the dead will be raised imperishable, and we will be changed. For the perishable must clothe itself with the imperishable, and the mortal with immortality. When

the perishable has been clothed with the imperishable, and the mortal with immortality, then the saying that is written will come true: "Death has been swallowed up in victory."

"Where, O death, is your victory?

"Where, O death, is your sting?"

The sting of death is sin, and the power of sin is the law. But thanks be to God! He gives us the victory through our Lord Jesus Christ (1 Corinthians 15:51–57).

Because of all that God has done through the transactions of grace, we are brought into a new—a victorious—relationship with Him. We find ourselves living in awe of His love, His compassion, and His grace. And the more we love Him, the more we want to serve Him—to share our days and our nights with Him. Paul brings us face to face with this reality when he tells us that "Christ's love compels us, because we are convinced that one died for all, and therefore all died. And he died for all, that those who live should no longer live for themselves but for him who died for them and was raised again" (2 Corinthians 5:14, 15). Paul goes on to share the fact that when we come face to face with Jesus, the transformation that follows positions us for eternity. "I want to know Christ—yes, to know the power of his resurrection and participation in his sufferings, becoming like him in his death, and so, somehow, attaining to the resurrection from the dead" (Philippians 3:10, 11).

The fact is that all of us are sinners. And all too often we focus upon who we are and where we have been and then we become discouraged and even depressed. Ellen White shares a great insight with us in her little book *Steps to Christ*. She tells us that we are not to "look to yourself, not to let the mind dwell upon self, but look to Christ. Let the mind dwell upon His love, upon the beauty, the perfection, of His character. Christ in His self-denial, Christ in His humiliation, Christ in His purity and holiness, Christ in His matchless love—this is the subject for the soul's contemplation. It is by loving Him, copying Him, depending wholly upon Him, that you are to be transformed into His likeness."[1]

It is very possible that as you are reading this book, you are silently struggling with some negative behavior—some habit of sin that has you so tightly bound up that you may have given up. You may have concluded that you will never be saved. Here is more great news from Paul—again from 2 Corinthians 5:21: You are not alone, and you don't have to give up in despair. Jesus has conquered sin! Here's what that means to those who are battling sin: Jesus has "disarmed the powers and authorities, he made a public spectacle of them, triumphing over them by the cross" (Colossians 2:15).

What you and I cannot do, Jesus did!

"Therefore, there is now no condemnation for those who are in Christ Jesus, because through Christ Jesus the law of the Spirit who gives life has set you free from the law of sin and death. For what the law was powerless to do because it was weakened by the flesh, God did by sending his own Son in the likeness of sinful flesh to be a sin offering. And so he condemned sin in the flesh, in order that the righteous requirement of the law might be fully met in us, who do not live according to the flesh but according to the Spirit" (Romans 8:1–4).

We observe this great exchange, and we hold our breath as we watch Jesus enter into a showdown with sin and eternal death—your death and mine! We see and we celebrate, because He wins! We cannot help but acknowledge that He has done what we never could have done. We give Him all praise and glory, and all our so-called glory is removed. Ellen White makes a very clear statement on this when she ponders this subject: "What is justification by faith? It is the work of God in laying the glory of man in the dust, and doing for man *that which it is not in his power to do for himself.* When men see their own nothingness, they are prepared to be clothed with the righteousness of Christ."[2]

Just as we follow Him through the valley of the shadow of death and watch Him die for us, so He invites us to live a life that is beyond the grave both now and in the future. He wants us to place our faith in His power to win and not in our own abilities.

I am always amazed by the Strongman Competition. This event brings competitors from around the world. Athletes flip cars, pull trucks, lift four-hundred-pound stones, and flip one-thousand-pound tires. The typical athlete, at six feet three inches tall and 330 pounds, with twenty-three-inch biceps and a fifty-eight-inch chest is more like a superhero than a professional athlete. I have even seen them pull jets. It is mind-boggling to me because there are times when I am thrilled just to be able to carry my own body around for a full day!

However, you and I have the privilege of experiencing even greater power. We have the privilege of understanding "the exceeding greatness of His power toward us who believe, according to the working of His mighty power which He worked in Christ when He raised Him from the dead and seated Him at His right hand in the heavenly places" (Ephesians 1:19, 20, NKJV). Please contemplate the following words: "Then one of the elders asked me, 'These in white robes—who are they, and where did they come from?' I answered, 'Sir, you know.' And he said, 'These are they who have come out of the great tribulation; they have washed their robes and made them white in the blood of the Lamb'" (Revelation 7:13, 14).

As a result of Jesus' life, death, and resurrection, He says to us, "The victory that I have accomplished over sin and eternal death is yours—you can have it just for the asking." Amazing! Sufficient enough! We find it all in Him.

Earlier in our examination of the passage in 2 Corinthians, we asked the painful question, "When God viewed Jesus on the cross, just what did He see?" We were constrained to answer this most painful question by saying that God saw the embodiment of your sins and mine. What a horrible thought that the pure and noble Jesus would be dragged down into the muck, and that His character would wind up resembling mine.

However, at this point, we need to ask another question. When God comes to the point of judgment and He reviews your case and mine, what does He see? He sees the beautiful life, death, and resurrection of Jesus. He sees Jesus' character, not mine! As I accept the transactions of grace, I ask God to cover me with the righteous character of His Son—and He does it! I embrace that by faith and walk in a new way—with new joy in my heart. Is that not the most amazing thought?

A professor was driving to work one morning and thinking about anything but the speed he was traveling. However, there was a watchful eye following him, and soon he became aware of it. The professor was pulled off to the side of the road and presented with a speeding ticket. Sad to say, this was not the first time that he had experienced being pulled over.

But as badly as he felt about the interchange, he pulled back onto the freeway and made his way home, thinking that he would pay the fine and that life would go on. However, sometime later he received a notice in the mail that shook him into a new reality. He was being summoned to court in order to defend his right to drive.

Weeks later, as he stood before the judge, his world caved in. "I am suspending your license for a period of one month," the judge intoned. "Your repeated infractions leave me with no alternative."

Still in a state of shock, the professor pled with the judge to reconsider the sentence and exchange it for a community-service-oriented penalty. "Your honor," he said, "I need my vehicle to make my livelihood, and if I cannot drive, I cannot work."

After some moments, the reasonable judge pronounced a new sentence, one more in line with the request of the professor. "I am giving you one month to clean up a one-mile section of the freeway adjacent to the university at which you teach." And with that, the trial was over.

Unfortunately, most of us understand from experience

what happened next. The professor procrastinated until the last moment. He went to the courthouse just prior to the end of the month and was granted a two-week extension. Then he returned home and got busy again—procrastinating.

On the day prior to the end of the second sentence, our professor headed out to the road to clean his mile. However, when he arrived, he discovered that the road had already been cleared and cleaned. He was amazed at how meticulously it had been done.

With a heavy heart and a sense of dread, he made his way home. As he turned into the driveway and pressed on the garage door remote control, he was shaken by what he saw. As the door lifted, he was looking directly into the back of his wife's station wagon—which was filled with garbage bags. His wife had cleaned the road.

I will never forget hearing this story and seeing the professor with tears in his eyes. He told us that the scene before him became a watershed moment for him. He sat in his driveway crying and praising God. And as he shared it all with us, he concluded, "This is what Jesus did for you and me. He took the garbage so that you and I could have eternal freedom from a penalty that was justifiably ours."

When we examine this story and ponder the words of Paul in 2 Corinthians 5:21, we come face to face with the phenomenal gift of God. It is His grace—His amazing grace—that provides all that we need, now and eternally! Let me tell you plainly: Jesus is enough for you and for me.

This gospel of Jesus is such a wonderful truth. And the exciting thing about it is that He has invited us to participate in it.

We are called to let this "Jesus of the exchange" change us. He invites us to place our lives in His hands so that we can see as He sees and act as He acts and treat one another as He treats us.

He is enough! We need nothing more!

Questions for Reflection and Discussion

1. Some people live so close to Jesus that we really can see Him in them. At times the example they give us may seem clearer and more in touch with our times and circumstances than Jesus' example is. What help can their witness be to us? What dangers does it pose?

2. This chapter notes that Ellen White wrote that justification by faith means God does for us what we can't do for ourselves. What is it that we can't do for ourselves?

3. Returning again to the great exchange, we see first of all that when God looks at the cross, He sees Jesus taking on the role of a sinner dying for his or her sins. The exchange, then, means that when God looks at those who are trusting in Him for their salvation, He sees them as having Jesus' sinless character and His perfect, unselfish life. If God truly sees us in this way, how will He treat us? Can we look for Him to be as happy and proud of us as human parents are of their children? Do we act as though we believe God views us this way? What effect does this have on those close to us?

Endnotes

1. Ellen G. White, *Steps to Christ*, 71.
2. White, *Manuscript Releases* (Silver Spring, Md.: E. G. White Estate, 1993), 20:117; italics added.

Chapter 18

Enough for the Future

I t was one of those moments in life when I truly would have liked to have found a hole, crawled into it, and then pulled the hole in after me. *What do words do at times like this?* I thought. As I sat there in stunned silence, searching for words to put together, one of the women sitting in the backseat of the car with the three children proceeded to tell them that their mother had been killed.

Their parents had gone grocery shopping on a motorcycle. As they moved through a large crowd on a busy street of Pune, India, a truck engine backfired, frightening a woman in the crowd. She lunged forward, pushing the motorcycle and both riders over—killing the dear mother. It was a terrible tragedy.

As this horrendous news fell on the ears of the stunned children, the oldest of the three blurted out in agony, "Then who will read us our story before we go to bed?"

What pain! Who is going to take care of our needs? Who is going to pray with us and for us? Who will take care of us in the future? The cry of that young girl reverberates throughout human experience!

Whatever your life circumstance, this question is always there, lurking ominously in our minds. Whether you have been abused or privileged, rich or poor, brilliant, average, or a slow learner, we all face the same question: What about the future?

Could we become so preoccupied with the future that we develop a personal paranoia about it? Yes. However, there is good news. God is deeply interested in your future and mine. He assures us that He is planning for us to be around in His future, saying plainly, "I know the plans I have for you, . . . plans to prosper you and not to harm you, plans to give you hope and a future" (Jeremiah 29:11). He who does not lie also tells us that He will not abandon us. He says, "I will never leave you nor forsake you" (Joshua 1:5). And Jesus affirms this nonabandonment promise when He says, "Surely I am with you always, to the very end of the age" (Matthew 28:20). So, though you and I cannot see beyond the veil that hides the future, the fact is that we know who is going with us into that future.

There is also an event that all of us face. It is the amazing return of Jesus to this earth. We can have confidence that even at that time, Jesus will take care of our needs. The Word of God assures us that we do not have to fear as we face the future and Jesus' second coming. As a matter of fact, Jesus offers strong assurances as He speaks of His return. He says, "Let not your heart be troubled; you believe in God, believe also in Me. In My Father's house are many mansions; if it were not so, I would have told you. I go to prepare a place for you. And if I go and prepare a place for you, I will come again and receive you to

Myself; that where I am, there you may be also" (John 14:1–3, NKJV).

So your role and mine is to keep our eyes fixed upon the All-Sufficient One—to believe in God and in Jesus. We can have confidence that the One who created us will also save us. "So do not throw away your confidence; it will be richly rewarded. You need to persevere so that when you have done the will of God, you will receive what He has promised. For, 'In just a little while, he who is coming will come and will not delay' " (Hebrews 10:35–37).

In December 1981, our family waited in the observation deck of Katanayake Airport outside of Colombo, Sri Lanka, for the arrival of my mother and stepfather. They were coming to spend a month with us, and all of us had a huge sense of anticipation.

We heard the jet land, so we were expecting to see them emerge from the security lines at any moment. However, there was a lengthy delay. My stepfather had left his wallet on the aircraft, and there was the proverbial red tape to go through to get it back. But we were almost beginning to lose hope—and we would have if it weren't for the fact that I had read the flight manifest. They had to be on that jet. And sure enough, after some time they appeared, and we rejoiced.

Jesus will return. God says He will, and His Word points to many signs. We have read the flight manifest, so to speak, and it makes clear that our Lord Jesus will return. One day soon all of the prophetic signs will be fulfilled and we will see Him.

What will it be like to see Him come? The conclusion of the book *The Great Controversy* has always been a blessing to me. It pictures in graphic detail the scene of Jesus' return. How it thrills me to read that description of your Savior and mine returning to take us to be with Him forever.

> Soon there appears in the east a small black cloud, about half the size of a man's hand. It is the cloud which surrounds the Saviour and which seems in the distance to be shrouded in darkness. The people of God know this to be the sign of the Son of man. In solemn silence they gaze upon it as it draws nearer the earth, becoming lighter and more glorious, until it is a great white cloud, its base a glory like consuming fire, and above it the rainbow of the covenant. Jesus rides forth as a mighty conqueror. Not now a "Man of Sorrows," to drink the bitter cup of shame and woe, He comes, victor in heaven and earth, to judge the living and the dead. . . . No human pen can portray the scene; no mortal mind is adequate to conceive its splendor.[1]

In the book *Early Writings,* we have another wonderful description of the redemption of the redeemed: "We tried to call up our greatest trials, but they looked so small compared with the far more exceeding and eternal weight of glory that surrounded us that we could not speak them out, and we all cried out, 'Alleluia, heaven is cheap enough!' and we touched our glorious harps and made heaven's arches ring."[2]

And then the saved all cry out with one voice to our precious Jesus: "You are worthy, our Lord and God, to receive glory and honor and power, for you created all things, and by your will they were created and have their being." "Worthy is the Lamb, who was slain, to receive power and wealth and wisdom and strength and honor and glory and praise!" (Revelation 4:11; 5:12). In the midst of these pictures of praise, John writes, "Then I heard every creature in heaven and on earth and under the earth and on the sea, and all that is in them, saying: 'To him who sits on the throne and to the Lamb be praise and honor and glory and power, for ever and ever!' " (Revelation 5:13).

Because Jesus' life, death, and resurrection have fulfilled the will of God in every sense, there will come a time of universal acknowledgment of this. Paul puts it like this: "God exalted him [Jesus] to the highest place and gave him the name that is above every name, that at the name of Jesus every knee should bow, in heaven and on earth and under the earth, and every tongue acknowledge that Jesus Christ is Lord, to the glory of God the Father" (Philippians 2:9–11).

One day soon the entire universe will proclaim the truth: Jesus is enough!

Questions for Reflection and Discussion

1.   What frightens you most about the near future? What about the distant future? What promises has Jesus given us to provide us with assurance no matter what we may have to face?

2.   What gives you hope that Jesus will be true to His word and return to this earth to take us to live with Him throughout eternity?

3.   Do you have the assurance that despite your weakness and sin, when Jesus returns, He'll call you to His side? Jesus wants us to have that assurance—to trust His sufficiency, to rest in the

salvation He can provide. It's our privilege to live our lives within that assurance. Why not accept it today—now?

Endnotes

1. Ellen G. White, *The Great Controversy* (Nampa, Idaho: Pacific Press®, 2005), 640, 641.
2. White, *Early Writings* (Washington, D.C.: Review and Herald®, 1945), 17.